WHERE HUMAN RIGHTS & BIBLICAL JUSTICE MEET

Imago Dei & Integral Mission

EDITED BY STEVE BRADBURY

EASTERN COLLEGE AUSTRALIA   GRACEWORKS

Where Human Rights & Biblical Justice Meet

Imago Dei & Integral Mission

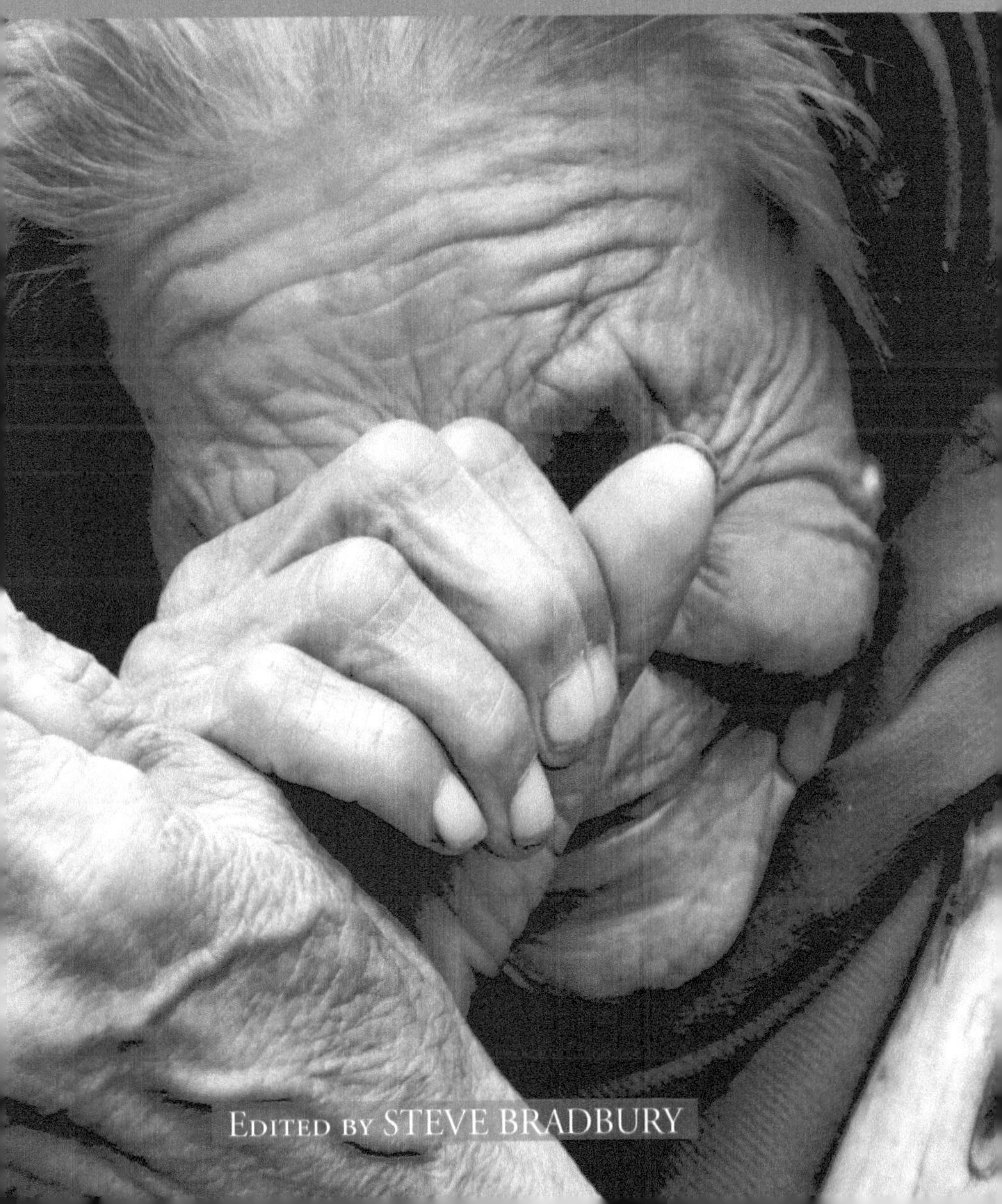

Edited by STEVE BRADBURY

These nine essays challenge our understanding of the Bible and compel us to rethink how theology should be applied in the context of the human condition. They confront the reality of everyday life, from the status of patriarchy, gender equality and egalitarianism, to mobility and employment, human trafficking and modern day slavery, to social security, land rights and the displacement of the urban poor, to community participation in decision-making and development, and to the appropriate origins, foundations and norms in the advocacy for and promotion of human rights values. In the quest to speak truth to power, what should be the proper role of Christian counter-culture in the engagement amongst Scripture, human rights, justice, fairness and political systems? Be prepared for an upending of conventional views, an upsetting of traditional values, and an unseating from our comfort zones.

Andrew Khoo
Advocate and Solicitor of the High Court of Malaya in Malaysia,
Co-Chair Human Rights Committee, Bar Council of Malaysia, 2011–2018,
Chancellor (Legal Advisor) to the Anglican Bishop of West Malaysia (2001–present),
Chancellor to the Anglican Archbishop of South East Asia (2012–2020)

Where Human Rights & Biblical Justice Meet is a wonderful, stirring and challenging collection of essays. The contributors take Biblical teaching thousands of years old and really wrestle with it and apply it to very real, raw and live current situations of injustice and human rights abuses in our world today. They find challenge, wisdom, hope and power for us as the church/Christians seek to shine God's truth and life and bring change into some of the world's darkest situations of injustice.

Paul Cook
Head of Advocacy, Tearfund UK

These essays provide a firsthand insight into a wide range of human rights issues from Nepal to Indonesia. They would be a useful resource to anyone looking to respond, to complex problems that nations face, with God's heart and wisdom.

Tehmina Arora
General Secretary, Christian Legal Association of India

Contents

Contributors

Steve Bradbury is Course Coordinator for Eastern College Australia's Master of Transformational Development. Prior to joining Eastern's faculty in 2009, he served as the National Director of TEAR Australia (1984–2009), the inaugural Chair of Micah Global (1999–2009), and the International Board of Micah Challenge (2003–4, 2008–12).

Julie Bellingham currently lives in New Delhi, India with her husband and four kids and works in Communications for a Christian NGO—The Evangelical Fellowship of India Commission on Relief. She is passionate about engaging with issues of injustice and poverty, and in assisting the church in the task of building a compassionate and just society.

Clinton Bergsma manages international partner relations for Amos Australia. He enjoys considering the practical implications of the kingdom of God and exploring the undeclared theologies that underpin the way we live and act.

Lyn Jackson loves to tell stories, especially about the creativity and resilience of ordinary people trapped in poverty, and about the God who expresses His care for them through His people. Lyn has worked as an educator and communications professional in Christian development agencies in India and Nepal, and also in Australia, seeking to encourage Christians to be part of God's global mission of compassion and justice.

LEE SOO CHOO is currently Programme Manager at Community Transformation Initiative, a small non-profit in Kuala Lumpur. After learning to walk with "two feet of love" in Malaysia and Afghanistan, she is still striving to be at the place where her deep gladness and the world's deep hunger meet.

KAREN LIM is a Programme Consultant with the Norwegian Mission Alliance, currently based in Cambodia with her husband and three boys. She lives her life in many tensions, navigating between different worlds, and is constantly disturbed by injustice and poverty. She enjoys thinking what God might have to say about this messy world and believes that we have a mandate to join Him in His mission, wherever we might be!

PETER LOCKWOOD is an engineer from Northern Ireland whose love affair with Nepal began in the late 1980s. Previously engaged in developing hydropower and industrial development capacity in Nepal, since 2012 he has been involved in leadership and programme management with a Christian Faith-based Organisation seeking to address the root causes of poverty in Nepal.

ARLENE WARD is a photographer and visual artist living and working in Vanuatu. She partners with various community groups and organisations in creative communication and attempts to use a little goodness, truth and beauty to inspire the world's wealthy towards action on justice-related issues.

MANU WARD and his family served with Servants to Asia's Urban Poor for four years in Indonesia, living in a squatter community of rubbish-pickers and engaging with them in grass-roots development initiatives. He now lives in Wellington, New Zealand, where he divides his time between civil engineering and church-based community development as a member of the Anglican missional order, Urban Vision.

INTRODUCTION

Steve Bradbury

Many years ago I had the good fortune to spend several days in a remote rural community on the banks of a majestic river in south-west Bangladesh—a place so rich in natural beauty, yet home to so many people beleaguered by economic poverty. An encounter with one of them left an indelible impression on me.

I had been invited to a meeting of participants in a women's empowerment programme, and I sat and listened as they told me of their efforts to create a better future for themselves and their children. They then asked me to tell them a little about myself, and after briefly doing so I invited questions. Now, over 20 years later, I can't recall any of the questions except for one. A young mother looked me in the eye and asked: "How come you are so rich and we are so poor?"

The development practitioners who had worked so hard to encourage these women to set up the group in the first place were thrilled by the question. (But *they* didn't have to answer it!) To explain their excitement they told me that until recently, that young woman wouldn't have been able to look me directly in the eye, let alone ask such a direct and confronting question.

At one level, the answer was (and still is) an utterly simple one. "It is an accident of our birth," I replied. "You were born a woman into a poor rural Bangladeshi family. I was born a son into a middle-class family that migrated from Britain to New Zealand."

However, behind that answer lay a far more complex history: of power and exploitation, of opportunity and choice for some, and the near absence of opportunity and choice for others. It is the story of how injustice denies vast numbers of people the chance to live fulfilling and abundant lives.

In his brilliant book *Until Justice and Peace Embrace*, Nicholas Wolterstorff describes the manner in which the British used their superior weapons to take control of the region of which Bangladesh is now part, and proceeded to systematically destroy its economy and social structure. He writes:

> The British wanted from Bengal a cheap, competition-free source of raw materials and a monopolistic market for their own manufactured goods, and they got what they wanted. In the process they pushed Bangladesh decisively into the pit of underdevelopment.[1]

Any reasonable answer to the question posed to me by that young Bangladeshi woman would have included the complexities of history; of how, in the absence of constraints on the powerful, the weak are exploited and oppressed.

We who are not economically poor might shy away from such disturbing realities, but the Bible doesn't. Consider these words from Job 24:1–12 (MSG):

> But if Judgment Day isn't hidden from the Almighty,
>   why are we kept in the dark?
> There are people out there getting by with murder—
>   stealing and lying and cheating.
> They rip off the poor
>   and exploit the unfortunate,
> Push the helpless into the ditch,
>   bully the weak so that they fear for their lives.

---

1 Nicholas Wolterstorff, *Until Justice and Peace Embrace* (Grand Rapids, MI: William B. Eerdmans, 1983) 98.

> The poor, like stray dogs and cats,
>> scavenge for food in back alleys.
> They sort through the garbage of the rich,
>> eke out survival on handouts.
> Homeless, they shiver through cold nights on the street;
>> they've no place to lay their heads.
> Exposed to the weather, wet and frozen,
>> they huddle in makeshift shelters.
> Nursing mothers have their babies snatched from them;
>> the infants of the poor are kidnapped and sold.
> They go about patched and threadbare;
>> even the hard workers go hungry.
> No matter how backbreaking their labor,
>> they can never make ends meet.
> People are dying right and left, groaning in torment.
>> The wretched cry out for help
>> and God does nothing, acts like nothing's wrong!

Job is considered to be one of the earliest-written books in the Bible, but this description of both the circumstances of the economically poor and politically weak, and their primary causes, is as valid today as it was then. Lack of food, hopelessly inadequate shelter and housing, exploited workers being paid totally unjust wages, shortened lives, trafficked children—what a despicable litany of human suffering. And, it would seem, made all the worse by the apparent absence and silence of God.

What does Jesus think about the grief and suffering of the poor and marginalised?

And what would Jesus have us be and do in response to the grievous injustices of poverty? These are **sacred questions**, and at the very moment in which he publicly announced and defined the purpose of his mission Jesus said something of immense relevance to them:

> When he came to Nazareth, where he had been brought up, he went to the synagogue on the sabbath day, as was his custom. He stood up to read, and the scroll of the prophet Isaiah was given

to him. He unrolled the scroll and found the place where it was written:

"The Spirit of the Lord is upon me because he has anointed me to bring good news to the poor. He has sent me to proclaim release to the captives and recovery of sight to the blind, to let the oppressed go free, to proclaim the year of the Lord's favour."

And he rolled up the scroll, gave it back to the attendant, and sat down. The eyes of all in the synagogue were fixed on him. Then he began to say to them, "Today this scripture has been fulfilled in your hearing." (Luke 4:16–21)

In times past, and perhaps in some church contexts still today, it has been common to hear these words of Jesus spiritualised in such a way as to ignore or even deny their significance to the ongoing tragedy of poverty and oppression. But to do this is to ignore something both intriguing and profound that Jesus did with Isaiah 61:1–2a as he read it out loud in Nazareth's synagogue. He slipped in some crucial words from Isaiah 58:6 "…to let the oppressed go free".

Why? Why were these extra words inserted?

David Bosch, one of the most eminent missiologists of the twentieth century, offers a compelling explanation. He argues that it was done in order to emphasise something "which was apparently not sufficiently clearly expressed in Isaiah 61. The phrase 'to let the oppressed go free' has a distinctly social profile in Isaiah 58. It stands in the context of prophetic criticism of social discrepancies in Judah, of the exploitation of the poor by the rich."[2]

The Luke 4 passage tells us that Jesus was profoundly concerned about the physical and material well-being of those who were oppressed and exploited. It tells us that justice and mercy and material well-being—in the here and now—are integral to the good news he proclaimed. Jesus' stories of the Good Samaritan, the Rich Fool, the wedding feast, the great

---

2   David J. Bosch, *Transforming Mission: Paradigm Shifts in Theology of Mission 20th Anniversary Edition* (Maryknoll, NY: Orbis, 2011) 102.

banquet, the workers in the vineyard, the persistent widow and the callous judge, the rich man and Lazarus, the sheep & the goats—all proclaim God's heart for the oppressed and those in great need.

So many of Jesus' encounters and actions demonstrated this Divine concern: his engagement with Zacchaeus, the healing of the haemorrhaging woman, the rescue of the woman caught in adultery, his compassion towards the woman at the well in Samaria, his feeding of the hungry, his condemnation of pharisaic hypocrisy...the list goes on and on.

Jesus' actions and teaching are the greatest testimony of all to a core biblical truth that "the equality and intrinsic worth of all human beings" derives from the fact that "they are created in the image of God."[3] This is the foundation of human rights.

Each chapter in this book explores the implications of this truth for Christian mission, and each chapter started life as an essay written by its author in the pursuit of their Master of Transformational Development (MTD) at Eastern College Australia.[4] The authors all write out of their experience as transformational development practitioners—and they bring into the "academic space" of research and writing the lived experience and passion of vocation.

Steve Bradbury
Coordinator, Master of Transformational Development
Eastern College Australia

---

3   Vinoth Ramachandra, *Subverting Global Myths: Theology & the Public Issues Shaping Our World* (Downers Grove, IL: InterVarsity Press, 2008) 101.
4   See https://www.eastern.edu.au/courses/master-transformational-development

Gender Injustice in India and the Indian Church

Julie Bellingham

Discrimination against women and girls in India is widespread. Stories centring on rape, trafficking, dowry deaths, and child marriage often gain international media attention and reinforce India's reputation as being an unsafe place for women. One such story to hit world news headlines occurred in December 2012, when a 23-year-old student was gang-raped by six men on a moving bus and died 13 days later as a result of the injuries sustained during the incident. The comments made by one of the accused in a BBC documentary of the rape, titled *India's Daughter* (2015), reveal the accused's strong opinions in regards to the expected behaviour of women. He stated that, "Boys and girls are not equal. Housework and housekeeping is for girls, not roaming in bars and discos at night" (Udwin). He placed the responsibility of the rape with the victim, "A decent girl won't roam around at nine o'clock at night. A girl is far more responsible for rape than a boy" (Udwin, 2015b). He argued that her defensive actions made the situation worse, "She shouldn't fight back. She should just be silent and allow the rape" (Udwin, 2015b).

After surveying the extent of gender violence in India, this paper examines two of the underlying causes behind this phenomenon: the patriarchal system and the practice of dowry. The low status of women, in combination with the prevalence of gender violence, poses a challenge for the Indian church. If the church wishes to be a prophetic voice in this context, it must denounce gender violence, offer a biblical model of male-female relationships, and promote counter-cultural communities characterised by justice and righteousness. Adopting a biblical alternative vision of gender relationships requires that we recognise that both males and females are made in the image of God; they have equal worth and deserve equal opportunity to exercise their God-given abilities. I write this essay as a person of a different ethnicity, who lives in India. While this limits my understanding of the context and influences my perspective, my hope is that it may also give additional objectivity.

Gender Violence

Violence towards women in India occurs throughout the life course and begins in the womb with female foeticide and infanticide (Barik, 2014). Although it is illegal to do prenatal testing to determine gender, 12 million girls have been aborted over the last three decades (Barik, 2014:4–5). During childhood, girls are more likely than boys to experience neglect and under-nourishment, be denied education, and be married before they reach the age of 18 (Varkey, 2014). In both childhood and adulthood, females are vulnerable to rape, sexual harassment, abduction, trafficking, forced prostitution, domestic servitude and dowry death (National Crime Records Bureau, 2017). In 2016, India's rate of reported rape cases was 6.3 per 100,000 people. Although this number is not high by global standards, it has been claimed that 99 percent of incidents of violence towards women go unreported (Bhattacharya, 2018; Bandyopadhyay, 2018). Furthermore, as in the case mentioned above, the female is often blamed for sexual abuse (Barik, 2014). For many women, domestic violence is so commonplace that they do not expect anything different in their marriage and do not attempt to escape until the abuse becomes "utterly inhuman" (Nayak, 2017; Kudchedkar, 2013:9).

Obviously not all men in India express such sexist attitudes and neither are all women abused by their husbands or close relatives. Some women in India have exercised their freedom and have gained leadership positions in the corporate and public sectors (Koshy, 2007). Some have also managed to draw attention to the prevalence of sexual abuse by sharing their stories as part of the #MeToo campaign. However, leadership opportunity is not typical of the experience of the majority of Indian women, especially those from disadvantaged castes and those from rural areas (John, 2017). The experience of women in India differs significantly depending on their ethnicity, caste or class, age, religion, where they are located within the country, whether they are from an urban or a rural background, and whether their family is modern or traditional.

Gender-based violence is not unique to India. Many women in other countries can also tell stories of violence and abuse by men. However, when India's record is compared with many other countries it performs poorly and the situation is not improving (Livne, 2015). In 2018, India was ranked as the most dangerous country to be female, ahead of Afghanistan, Democratic Republic of Congo and Pakistan, by the Thomson Reuters Foundation global poll of gender experts. While the government has been reluctant to accept the findings of this poll, the United Nations Gender Development Index 2017 also confirmed the vulnerability of women in India, placing India in the fifth and lowest category (United Nations Development Programme, 2016:210–213). In addition, India performed poorly in *The Global Gender Gap Report 2018* ranking 108 out of 149 countries.

THE CAUSES OF GENDER VIOLENCE

Violence towards women in India can be linked to a myriad of factors, including, but not limited to, gender inequality, poverty, economic stress, cultural and religious traditions, powerlessness, the caste system, lack of implementation of laws, and ideas around masculinity (Udwin, 2015a; Lahiri, 2008). Law enforcement agencies are also culpable and have been accused of failure to carry out full investigations, failure to capture evidence, lack of urgency in investigating cases, and even raping women in their custody (Dubey, 2018). However, if gender violence was to be attributed to a few main causes, the patriarchal system and the practice of dowry would be key factors. In Priyanka Dubey's report on rape in India, she sums up the issue of gender violence, "Patriarchy is the nucleus of this problem and all other factors contributing to violence against women manifest themselves around it" (2018:viii).

Innately Patriarchal

Indian society and culture has been described as "innately patriarchal" (Vadalia, 2013). Patriarchy can be defined as the social system where male members of a society tend to assume and dominate positions of power, believing that the male is the head of the family or organisation (Varghese, 2013). These patriarchal values have established a clear division of roles in the Indian home and in Indian society, which effectively restrict the role, influence and opportunities of women. In many families, in workplaces, in religious settings, and in society, men enjoy authority, power and privilege (Bhattacharya, 2013). The man is considered to be the undisputed 'head of family' and he is likely to be the bread-winner, take charge of finances and in some cases do the 'outside work', such as shopping (Bhattacharya, 2013). Women are expected to submit to and serve their husbands. Some women do not have the freedom to pursue employment but find their role is limited to domestic duties and the raising of children (Livne, 2015:13).

Patriarchal values are taught to children from an early age. In childhood, girls are taught to be submissive and obedient, to conform to dress and behaviour codes, to stay at home as much as possible, to make personal sacrifices and to be tolerant and virtuous (Bhattacharya, 2013; Varghese & Jacob, 2017). Many consider formal education unnecessary for female children or they consider the education of daughters to be of a lower priority than the education of sons (Koshy, 2007). Single women are unlikely to live on their own, but instead live in the family home under the care of the father until they are married and then become the responsibility of their husband. They are taught to be subservient to their husbands and are expected to put the needs of the family before their own needs. Generally speaking, the patriarchal system in India sees that women are disempowered, dependent on their husbands or their families, and unable to exercise freedom in the full span of activities that make up their daily lives.

The patriarchal system draws its legitimacy from religious and cultural beliefs and practices (Bhattacharya, 2013). Despite the fact that in the Hindu religious tradition people worship female goddesses, "women at the ground level share no such glorified status" (Arya, 2013:35). There is a strong cultural tradition sanctioned by some religious texts of treating one's husband as god (Mondol, 2014:10–11; John, 2017). Additionally, according to the Laws of Manu, one of the most authoritative of the books of the Hindu code, women are expected to live in submission to male authority, "In childhood a female must be subject to her father, in youth to her husband, when her lord is dead to her sons. A woman must never be independent" (Arora, 2007:212). While women can make important contributions to Hindu religious life, they hold no religious authority (Arora, 2007). In contrast, a son carries forward the family name, performs burial rites, and inherits ancestral property (Arora, 2007). Unfortunately, when a woman receives a beating from her husband it is believed to be her misfortune, or her karma (Bhattacharya, 2013).

The Dowry System

The dowry system also contributes towards a culture of violence against women. Dowry is the traditional social practice whereby the bride's family gives cash, goods or property to the groom's family on their marriage. Despite the fact that dowry is prohibited, and has been since 1961, it maintains a significant presence in contemporary India amongst both disadvantaged and high-caste groups (Sharma, 2014). When the dowry is considered by the groom and his family to be inadequate, the bride's life can be made miserable (Varghese, 2013; John, 2017). In some cases, an inadequate dowry has led to violence towards women, humiliation, burning of the bride or suicide. In 2015, 21 women per day were either burnt alive or forced to commit suicide as a result of an inadequate dowry (according to The National Crime Records Bureau, Nigam, 2017).

Together the patriarchal system and the practice of dowry have "sanctioned an institutionalized system of male domination at many levels of Indian culture" (Varghese, 2013:41). The patriarchal system has established a hierarchical structure in India that has created inequality between men and women, and caused women to be regarded as inferior (Varghese, 2013). By placing men in authority over women, the patriarchal system has seen women become subordinate objects in a man's world. This is compounded by the practice of dowry, which has seen girls come to be associated with financial loss, while having a son is associated with financial gain (Barik, 2014). In an interview for *India's Daughter*, Sheila Dixit, Delhi Chief Minister (1998–2013) noted that, "Many of our people grow up thinking that a girl is less important than a boy" (Udwin, 2015b). Boys learn early in childhood that their needs have preference over those of their sisters. What then follows from this is the assumption that "because she is less important you can do what you like with her" (Sheila Dixit in Udwin, 2015b). Pal describes this as the socialisation of violence against women (Pal, 2016). For some women, the system of patriarchy and the practice of dowry has restricted their role in the home and society, for other women, they have been treated as commodities, slaves and liabilities in their own family (Pushpa Lalitha, 2017:81).

These perceptions of women are widely held. The director of the *India's Daughter* documentary, Leslee Udwin, stated that "the horrifying details of the rape had led me to expect deranged monsters. Psychopaths. The truth was far more chilling. These were ordinary, apparently normal and certainly unremarkable men" (2015a). A similar statement was made by Madhumita Pandey, who interviewed 100 rapists in India for her doctoral thesis (including the accused mentioned above), "I was convinced these men are monsters. But when you talk to them, you realize these are not extraordinary men, they are really ordinary. What they've done is because of upbringing and thought process" (Doshi, 2017). The educated and wealthy are also known to hold such views; the defence lawyer to the accused mentioned above, AP Singh, said that if his daughter had "disgraced herself" by doing such things that he would "put petrol on her and set her alight" in front of his entire family (Udwin, 2015a). These comments reveal a deeply entrenched patriarchal mind-set in India, which treats women as subordinate and places them in an extremely vulnerable position.

THE SITUATION IN THE INDIAN CHURCH

The subordinate status of women and the pervasiveness of gender abuse poses a challenge for the Indian church. Does the church in India mirror society or has it been able to foster a counter narrative that recognises the dignity and worth of both women and men? Do women have the freedom in the church setting to pursue their calling and offer their gifts for the well-being of the community?

Women in the Family

Gender-based violence is prevalent in Christian families in India. Thomas Varghese's 2013 study to ascertain the level, type and seriousness of abuse faced by women from their husbands in Christian families in India, found that Christian women are equally victims of gender-based violence. His study of 100 Christian women from nine denominations revealed that 92 percent of the respondents had experienced some form of abuse—psychological, verbal, physical, sexual, financial or social (Varghese, 2013:112). In Bonnie Jacob's recent study, "Gender Perceptions in the Churches and the Experiences of Women: A Case Study of Christians in Delhi", she found that approximately 20 percent to 30 percent of the 547 respondents were facing abuse at home and a further 20 percent were not categorical in stating whether they had been abused (Jacob, 2017:3). Manasseh's study of 80 middle- and upper-middle-class women revealed that 100 percent of the women had been hit or slapped and 50 percent had been beaten (Manasseh, 2007:192). Others have also confirmed that domestic abuse is commonplace in Christian homes (Mondol, 2014; Kumar, 2017; Koshy 2017; Wood, 2007). Varghese concludes that the church needs to be different, but "most of the time we are not different from others. Sometimes, we are worse than non-Christians" (Varghese, 2013:118).

The Indian Christian community practices what is called complementarianism. Complementarians do not doubt that women are equal spiritually and ontologically, but believe that the Bible requires different roles of women and men. Similar to patriarchal beliefs evident in the wider society, the husband is created to be the head of the family and the wife is expected to submit and assume a supportive role. According to complementarians, this ordering of the family is justified from scripture that refers to husbands as the 'head of the wife' and instructs wives to be subject and submissive (Eph. 5:21–6:9; 1 Cor. 11:3–16; Tit. 2:5; Col. 3:18 and 1 Pet. 3:1–7). Typically, in conservative Indian Christian households, the man retains full control over his wife and she is expected to come under his authority and respect his decisions (Varghese, 2013:69–70). When the wife is disobedient or fails to meet her husband's expectations, it is considered to be the husband's role and right as the head of the family to discipline his wife in whatever manner is deemed appropriate (Varghese, 2013; Kumar, 2017). Often, if a woman is beaten by her husband she is believed by those around her to have deserved it (Kumar, 2017). Women that have sought help from friends, relatives or pastors have been told to accept the situation, return to the husband and to remain silent (Wood, 2007:239; Barik, 2014:6). It is hard to determine the exact extent of abuse in Christian homes because many deny its existence, are too ashamed to admit it, fear the reaction of their husband, fear financial insecurity, or perceive it to be a private matter (Barik, 2014). Consequently, Christian women adopt the "Silent

Approach" or the "Acceptance Approach", accepting domestic violence as a part of life (Manasseh, 2007:195).

Women's Role in the Church

This gender division of roles is also evident in the church. In many churches, the role of women is confined to teaching Sunday School, teaching at women's meetings, preaching on "Women's Sunday" and being part of the worship team. It has been noted that in most Protestant denominations, church is a predominantly male-led experience, "there are either no women in leadership positions or their presence is negligible" (Arora, 2007:214).

> The stage in front was where the musicians, the preachers and their translators, and the elder who made announcements all took their turns. All were male. That was the way it was, and I never thought to ask why it should not be otherwise. (Havilah Dharamraj, 2017:70)

Male headship has been applied to the leadership of the church and consequently many Indian churches are led by male pastors, vicars and clergymen. Those that argue that only men can lead and preach (whether it be as a pastor, elder, deacon and in some cases worship leader) often point to 1 Timothy 2:8–15, which states that "no woman to teach or have authority over a man" and 1 Corinthians 14:34–35 where Paul says women "are not permitted to speak, but should be subordinate" (also refer to 1 Tim. 3:1–12). It is often not an issue that is much discussed, possibly due to its contentious nature, but also likely because it is commonly accepted as the way things are done. In *How I Changed my Mind about Women in Leadership* (2017), Nengzakhup recalled the ordination of women was a "non-issue", he never saw a woman preaching and "nobody even asked why" (2017:187). It is no surprise that Jacob's study (2017) found that over 60 percent of the 547 women interviewed stated that they have felt restricted because of their gender.

The church has failed to see its formative role in determining and preserving how its members understand gender, described by Jacob as "gender shaping" (Jacob, 2017). Jacob's study (2017) found that not many pastors perceived gender shaping to be crucial to Christian faith, therefore there was no intentionality about including this topic in their teaching or sermons. In *How I Changed my Mind about Women and Leadership*, John Kumar stated that as a child, if he had heard teaching from the pulpit against domestic violence, then he "would have known what to think" about the violence he observed in his family's home, but instead he felt troubled and confused (Kumar, 2017:25–27). Varghese's study (2013) revealed that the majority of clergymen and the church knowingly or unknowingly turns a blind eye to the abuse occurring in Christian families, believing it to be negligible, insignificant or unimportant (2003:3, 43). A likely side-effect of males filling teaching roles in the church is that there is an "unconscious bias" that fails to draw attention to the issues around gender, and consequently, further entrenches an environment that is prejudicial to women (Koshy, 2007:165).

More recently, some church denominations have permitted, or at least not forbidden, women to train in seminary and the ordination of women pastors. The Church of South India, in particular, has accepted women in leadership positions for the last 70 years. In 2013, it appointed Pushpa Lalitha as Bishop of the Nandyal Diocese, making Lalitha the first woman to be appointed as a bishop in the Church of South India. But while it may seem that some churches approve of women in leadership, being ordained has not necessarily guaranteed these women opportunities to preach or pastor a church (Cherian, 2017; Dutta, 2017:55). Sucheta Nayak, Registrar and a faculty lecturer at Mission India Theological Seminary in Nagpur, stated

> Often, even when I thought I was capable of doing something, I did not get a chance just because I am a woman. I had completed Bible study degrees, and my church could have been a platform for me to grow in faith and ministry experience, but they did not give me one chance to preach, not even until today (Nayak, 2017:179).

Jacob's study discovered that although a number of churches expressed egalitarian beliefs there was still a major gap between their stated policies and the actual opportunities that were given to women (Jacob, 2017:2).

Mirroring Society

The Indian church in many ways mirrors the patriarchal values and hierarchical structure that are evident in the wider society. There is no sense in the literature that Christian families differ remarkably from the wider Indian society in how their families are structured and in their expected roles. The patriarchal system places women—in both the church and in the wider society—in a vulnerable position, increasing their likelihood of experiencing prejudice, discrimination and abuse. Consequently, neither church nor society is free of violence towards women. Jacob's study (2015) concludes that the "hypothesis of the church being countercultural and a model for the rest of the society could not be sustained in the face of the considerable evidence otherwise" (2015:4). To say this in another way, the church is no exception to the comment that "prejudice towards women is entrenched in Indian culture" (Bhattacharya, 2013:14).

It is not unusual or extraordinary for the church to be influenced by its context, in fact as a cultural institution it is impossible for it not to be. The ever-present challenge for the global church is to discern whether it has adopted the beliefs and values of the local culture to the detriment of its mission and calling. The evidence of gender-based violence and inequality provides an opportunity for the Indian church to reflect on the assumptions it holds about the role of women, and to assess whether its theology and activities are building compassionate and just communities. The church has the task of prophetic ministry, which Walter Brueggemann defines as the task of "nurtur[ing], nourish[ing], and evok[ing] a consciousness and perception alternative to the consciousness and perception of the dominant culture around us" (Brueggemann, 2001). This requires that the church develops a consciousness of the dominant culture, including an awareness of the beliefs and values underlying common practices, and then to face the difficult task of honestly reflecting on its involvement in those practices. While the church must criticise and highlight the inadequacies of the dominant culture, it also has the task of imagining a biblical alternative and then energising people towards an alternative vision of the future (Brueggemann, 2001).

Towards an Alternative

Biblical Egalitarianism

If the church is to offer a prophetic voice, it is vital that the churches reach "a biblical and just theory and theology of the relation of women and men" (Wood, 2007:18). A Biblical egalitarian vision of male-female relationships, which highlights the biblical mandate for equality and the mutual submission of husband and wife, provides a theological foundation for equal rights and opportunities for men and women. Biblical exegesis that supports an egalitarian view of relationships is extensive and, generally speaking, highlights what is culturally relative and what constitutes trans-cultural truth in the scriptures (Howell, 2007:26). A few of the main arguments for a biblical egalitarian view are introduced below.

Both male and female are created in the image and likeness of God (Gen. 1:27–28) and are therefore equal in essence and being. Eve was described as a suitable helper (*ezer knegdo*) for Adam, a word that is also used to describe God Himself, and therefore cannot mean subordination (Saysell, 2017). This simple truth that both men and women are ontologically equal means that a woman cannot be regarded as inferior simply because she is a woman (Groothuis, 2004). Groothuis states that it is incoherent to argue that women are both ontologically equal *and* permanently, comprehensively and necessarily subordinate (Groothuis, 2004:304). Women are equal in essence and being, and therefore they do not "suffer from a net deficiency of the valuable qualities and inherent capacities distinctively characteristic of human nature and human behaviour" (Groothuis, 2004:307, 308). Women have the ability to participate alongside men in the various distinctively human activities, such as spiritual discernment, high-level cognitive/rational behaviours including decision-making skills, planning and problem solving (Groothuis, 2004). Equality in being demands that both women and men receive an "equality of consideration" and the opportunity to exercise their God-given abilities and work in their area of calling (Groothuis, 2004).

Jesus was radically different to contemporary rabbis and provides a model of treating women with dignity and respect. Although he had 12 male disciples, he also had women disciples—including Mary Magdalene, Joanna, and Susanna—who followed Him on his itinerant ministry and were integral to his discipleship team (Luke 8:1–3) (Harris, 2017a). Jesus approved of Mary sitting at his feet, a posture that at the time communicated that one was a disciple of a rabbi, and he commended Mary for her choice (Bailey, 2008). He not only instructed women, but commanded women to go and proclaim the news to the men (Matt. 28:10). Ross summarises Jesus' relationship with women,

> He discussed theology with women (the Samaritan woman at the well), he liberated women from bondage (the women with the issue of blood), he challenged gender bias (the woman caught in adultery), the first people he entrusted himself to after the resurrection were women, he had women among his disciples and was financially supported by them, he selected images and parables to communicate on a deep level with women as much as men (Ross, 2011).

The writings of Paul are often used as justification for the subordination of women to men, particularly his statement that the husband is the 'head' (*kephalē*) of his wife (Harris, 2017b). Often this verse is read through a contemporary lens; readers place themselves at the centre of the text and interpret the text according to their present-day ideas (Harris, 2017b:8). Dr Harris notes that while the word *kephalē* can mean a literal head on a body and "a being of high status", it was more often used in biblical times as the "source" or "origin" (Harris, 2017b:8). She notes that a complementarian reading of *kephalē* as a metaphor for leader is inadequate for the following reasons:

> Christian women are sustained by Christ; he is the one the woman submits to; he is her leader. The man plays no mediatory role for the woman; indeed, in orthodox theology neither he, nor any human can fulfil what Christ alone does. Women have the same access and accountability to Christ; and her spirituality is not mediated by another human; in Christ alone her hope is found; he is her rock, her strength, her song (Harris, 2017b:10).

Furthermore, to interpret *kephalē* as meaning "authority over" would mean that God has eternal authority over Christ, which borders on heresy (Harris, 2017b:10). Although Christ temporarily gave up equality with the Father when he lived on earth, he remains an equal part of the Trinity (Giles, 2007a). Christ is not eternally subordinate to the Father in function or authority, therefore the permanent subordination of women to men is not justified.

Paul operated within his cultural context. He was a first-century Jewish man who lived in a world that took both slavery and subordination of women for granted. In the book of Ephesians, Paul not only tells women to be subordinate to their husbands but exhorts slaves to obey and respect their masters. In our contemporary society, we no longer see Paul as condoning or endorsing slavery, but rather seeking to keep the peace and promote goodwill in a context where slavery was very firmly established and freedom seemed unattainable (Giles, 2017). By this rationale we should also not take Paul's exhortation to women to be submissive as "normative for all times and cultures" (Reiher, 2016:44). The exhortations to wives are "simply good practical advice to wives who had no other options" (Giles, 2017). It is also likely that Paul did not want female believers challenging traditional values and in doing so discrediting the word of God (Reiher, 2016:44).

It is also argued that in Timothy 2:8–15 Paul lays a blanket prohibition on all women from teaching men. But this interpretation isolates the scripture from its context (Reiher, 2016). A closer look at the wider picture reveals that the author of 1 and 2 Timothy also speaks of both women and men learning and teaching and describes a situation where the church was "under attack from false teachers" and women were involved (Reiher, 2016:42). Paul forbids these women from teaching because they had not been properly instructed and need further education in "sound doctrine" (Reiher, 2016). Therefore if this verse is seen in its context then it implies that it was "an exceptional situation" rather than a universal ruling (Reiher, 2016). In Paul's own ministry he ministered with women and allowed them significant roles in teaching (e.g. Phoebe, Junia, Priscilla, etc.) (Saysell, 2017). In fact, Giles argues that, given the cultural context, the number of women in leadership in the early Pauline churches is "breath-taking" (Giles, 2017).

A wider reading of Paul's writings and a closer look at the context suggest that Paul was somewhat counter-cultural. In Galatians 3:28 we read, "There is no longer Jew or Greek, there is no longer slave or free, there is no longer male or female; for all of you are one in Christ Jesus". While these distinctions continue to exist, they should not influence how we relate to others in the church (Seysall, 2017). God's gift of salvation and his call to discipleship are open to all, regardless of gender or ethnicity and socio-economic class. This should transform our relationships with others and encourage us to fight against any form of discrimination (Reiher, 2016:46).

Paul's view on how husbands and wives should relate to each other was counter-cultural for his context. In 12 instances in this Bible passage "he makes the opportunities, rights and privileges of the man and woman exactly the same" (Giles, 2017). Paul wrote "For the wife does not have authority over her own body, but the husband does; likewise the husband does not have authority over his own body, but the wife does" (1 Cor. 7:4–6). This placed husbands and wives on equal footing and was revolutionary teaching in a patriarchal culture that saw wives as the property of their husbands (Dutta, 2017:53). Paul asked husbands, as well as wives, to "Be subject to one another out of reverence to Christ" (Eph. 5:21). He also subverted patriarchy by exhorting husbands to sacrificially serve their wives, and to love their wives, "just as Christ loved the church and gave himself up for her" (Eph. 5:25) (Giles, 2017).

Responding to Gender Violence and Building Equality

In the Family

Modelling equality and mutual respect in the family is a key place to start in nourishing a biblically based alternative culture. A common factor behind the development of egalitarian views on women in leadership in a significant number of the stories told in *How I Changed My Mind about Women in Leadership* (2017) was being part of a family where the mother or the wife took some form of leadership in the family, demonstrating the capability of women and challenging traditional and cultural assumptions in regards to gender. However, for transformation to take place there also needs to be the involvement of husbands and fathers. In order to end gender-based violence and to create families where there is biblical equality it is necessary for men and women to submit to one another, to encourage each other to use their gifts and abilities, and to resolve conflict peacefully. Beulah Wood asks couples, "Do we submit to the other in mutual respect?", "Do we as wife and husband make family decisions together as joint members of the kingdom of God and co-heirs with Christ?" (2017:222). Our children will learn how to relate to the opposite gender through the example we set in the home. As parents, we must teach our sons that girls are their equals, made in the image of God and deserving of respect. Parents should treat sons and daughters alike and have equal expectations of both. Wood asks parents, "Do we invest equally in the education and future of daughters and sons, and enable both to make important decisions such as career and marriage in their own right before God?" (2017:222). Asking each other these questions is important if we want to see transformed relationships in the home.

In the Church

Aside from discussing theology, the church must examine the actual opportunities that are available to women, as well as the barriers that work to prevent women's involvement. The church needs to reflect a biblical perspective on gender by empowering women in the church and giving them the opportunity to fill leadership positions (Varkey, 2013). There needs to be an intentional decision on the part of church leadership to encourage women to train in pastoring and theological studies, to equally consider them for leadership roles, and then to ensure that they have opportunities to gain experience in leadership and preaching. Where there is an absence of women in specific roles, the responsibility is on the leadership to examine the factors that prevent women from filling these positions. It is also important to ensure that expectations held of women in leadership are realistic. We cannot expect women with little or no experience in preaching or leading to become sudden experts, nor should we compare their efforts to males with many years of experience. We also cannot expect women to necessarily lead in an identical manner to those of their male counterparts.

As followers of Christ, we cannot ignore gender-based violence that is occurring in Christian homes and in the wider society. The church has a role to highlight and speak against discrimination, oppression and violence towards women. The true worship that God desires is when we join with Him to "loose the bonds of injustice, to undo the thongs of the yoke, to let the oppressed go free, and to break every yoke" (Isa. 58:6). If the church is to act justly (Mic. 6:8) in regards to gender-based violence, there needs to be regular sermons condemning domestic abuse in order to send a clear message that such behaviour is not biblical (Varghese, 2013). The church has a responsibility to educate its members on the consequences of such behaviour and to teach its members to view and treat women with dignity and respect (Mondol, 2014:11). Church members need to be trained to recognise the signs of domestic abuse and be taught how to respond to abusive situations in their families and communities. If we can commit to treating each other with dignity and standing up against injustice then there is the hope that we can "influence further communities for righteousness" (Wood, 2007:18). As followers of Christ we can use our political voice to work towards change in the attitudes, the practices and the structures in society that prevent women from participating in life-giving communities.

> We in the church, set free by Christ, can be an example to the rest of our country. Sharing the good news of Jesus should go hand-in-hand with living and teaching equality, mutual respect, love and togetherness between the genders. I am hopeful of change. (Koshy & Thomas, 2017:130)

Conclusion

The patriarchal system and the practice of dowry have created a culture where women have come to be widely considered as inferior to men. This in turn has legitimatised the use of violence against women, girl children and even girl foetuses, as seen in the number of rapes, dowry deaths, female foeticide, domestic abuse, trafficking and kidnapping cases. The church also operates from a patriarchal perspective and in asserting strict gender roles, it too, has restricted the involvement of women in the home and in the church. Not only has this prevented Christian women from filling leadership roles in the church setting, but it has contributed towards creating violent and abusive family situations. Unfortunately, the Christian community is not remarkably different from the surrounding culture. If the church is to influence society towards righteousness, it must develop a consciousness of the dominant culture, acknowledge its complicity and then imagine and nourish a biblically-based alternative. A biblical model of male-female relationships, where both women and men are considered equal in being and essence, and where both are given the opportunity to participate freely in community, provides hope in a context where women are often treated as unwanted possessions.

REFERENCES

Arora, Tehmina. 2007. "Religion Law and Actualities in India." Pp. 211–218 in *Side by Side: Gender from a Christian Perspective*, edited by B. Wood. Bangalore, India: SAIACS Press.

Arya, Anwesha. 2013. "Devi: The Disempowered Goddess." Pp. 35–50 in *Behind Closed Doors: Domestic Violence in India*, edited by R. Bhattacharya. New Delhi, India: SAGE Publications India.

Bailey, Kenneth E. 2008. *Jesus Through Middle Eastern Eyes: Cultural Studies in the Gospels.* Downers Grove, IL: InterVarsity Press.

Barik, Bindulata. 2014. "Violence Against Women." Pp. 3–6 in *Drishkitone: Violence Against Women*, edited by EFICOR.

Bhattacharya, Pramit & Kundu, Tadit. 2018. "99% Cases of Sexual Assaults Go Unreported, Govt Data Shows." Retrieved February 6, 2020 (https://www.livemint.com/Politics/AV3sIKoEBAGZozALMX8THK/99-cases-of-sexual-assaults-go-unreported-govt-data-shows.html)

Bhattacharya, Rinki. 2013. "Introduction." Pp. 13–34 in *Behind Closed Doors: Domestic Violence in India*, edited by R. Bhattacharya. New Delhi, India: SAGE Publications India.

Brueggemann, Walter. 2001. *The Prophetic Imagination.* Minneapolis, MN: Fortress Press.

Chandy, K. 2007. "No Male Gods." Pp. 47–58 in *Side by Side: Gender from a Christian Perspective*, edited by B. Wood. Bangalore, India: SAIACS Press.

Cherian, Jacob. 2017. "Was Paul Against Women in Leadership in the Church?" Pp. 93–104 in *How I Changed my Mind about Women in Leadership: 20+ Indian Leaders Speak*, edited by B. Wood. Bangalore, India: SAIACS Press.

Dharamraj, H. 2017. "From Schoolgirl to Seminarian." Pp. 69–78 in *Side by Side: Gender from a Christian Perspective*, edited by B. Wood. Bangalore, India: SAIACS Press.

Doshi, Vidhi. 2017. "A Woman Interviewed 100 Convicted Rapists in India. This is What She Learned." Retrieved February 6, 2020 (https://www.washingtonpost.com/news/worldviews/wp/2017/09/11/a-woman-interviewed-100-convicted-rapists-in-india-this-is-what-she-learned/?utm_term=.4958b677ce09)

Dubey, Priyanka. 2018. *No Nation for Women.* New Delhi, India: Simon & Schuster.

Dutta, S. 2017. "Side by Side: Changing Worldviews on Leadership." Pp. 49–58 in *How I Changed my Mind about Women in Leadership: 20+ Indian Leaders Speak*, edited by B. Wood. Bangalore, India: SAIACS Press.

Ghosh, S.V. 2013. "Contextualizing Family Violence: Family, Community, State." Pp. 51–66 in *Behind Closed Doors: Domestic Violence in India*, edited by R. Bhattacharya. New Delhi, India: SAGE Publications India.

Giles, K. 2007. "Headship in Paul's Epistles." Pp. 143–160 in *Side by Side: Gender from a Christian Perspective*, edited by B. Wood. Bangalore, India: SAIACS Press.

---. 2007. "The Trinity and Subordinationism." Pp. 35–46 in *Side by Side: Gender from a Christian Perspective*, edited by B. Wood. Bangalore, India: SAIACS Press.

---. 2017. "Paul and Women: Was the Apostle a Misogynist?" Retrieved February 6, 2020 (https://www.cbe.org.au/index.php/articles/conferences/172-paul-and-women-was-the-apostle-a-misogynist)

Groothuis, R.M. 2004. "Equal in Being Unequal in Role: Exploring the Logic of Women's Subordination." Pp. 301–322 in *Discovering Biblical Equality: Complementarity without Hierarchy*, edited by R.W. Pierce, R.M. Groothuis & G.D. Fee. Downers Grove, IL: InterVarsity Press.

Harris, S. 2017a. "Jesus and Women." *Women and Ministry in the Church: Resource for the Baptist Churches of New Zealand*, edited by C. Saysell, S. Harris, S. & E. Rice. Retrieved February 6, 2020 (http://www.lifelonglearning.nz/images/Documents/Exegesis-of-Women-and-Ministry-in-the-Church.pdf)

Harris, S. 2017b. "Toward an Understanding 1 Corinthians 11:2–16." *Women and Ministry in the Church: Resource for the Baptist Churches of New Zealand*, edited by C. Saysell, S. Harris, S. & E. Rice. Retrieved February 6, 2020 (http://www.lifelonglearning.nz/images/Documents/Exegesis-of-Women-and-Ministry-in-the-Church.pdf)

Howell, R. 2007. "Gender from a Christian Perspective: Reflections from the Trinitarian Nature of God." Pp. 25–34 in *Side by Side: Gender from a Christian Perspective*, edited by B. Wood. Bangalore, India: SAIACS Press.

Jacob, B. 2017. Gender Perceptions in the Churches and the Experiences of Women: A Case Study of Christians in Delhi. Unpublished Paper presented by Dr. Bonnie Jacob on March 8, 2017.

John, N. 2017. "Three Factors Impacted my Understanding of Women." Pp. 193–202 in *How I Changed my Mind about Women in Leadership: 20+ Indian Leaders Speak*, edited by B. Wood. Bangalore, India: SAIACS Press.

Koshy, A & Koshy, O. 2017. "Mother Did What People Thought was a Man's Role." Pp. 39–48 in *How I Changed my Mind about Women in Leadership: 20+ Indian Leaders Speak*, edited by B. Wood. Bangalore, India: SAIACS Press.

Koshy, J. 2007. "Does Gender Define Roles?" Pp. 161–170 in *Side by Side: Gender from a Christian Perspective*, edited by B. Wood. Bangalore, India: SAIACS Press.

Koshy, J. & Thomas, C. 2017. "Two Equal Halves." Pp. 115–132 in *How I Changed my Mind about Women in Leadership: 20+ Indian Leaders Speak*, edited by B. Wood. Bangalore, India: SAIACS Press.

Kudchedkar, S. 2013. "Foreword." Pp. 9–10 in *Behind Closed Doors: Domestic Violence in India*, edited by R. Bhattacharya. New Delhi, India: SAGE Publications India.

Kumar, J.A. 2017. "Women are the Unsung Heroes." Pp. 19–30 in *How I Changed my Mind about Women in Leadership: 20+ Indian Leaders Speak*, edited by B. Wood. Bangalore, India: SAIACS Press.

Lahiri, D. 2008. "International Human Rights Standards: How Does India Measure Up?" Retrieved February 6, 2020 (http://cf.orfonline.org/wp-content/uploads/2008/05/IssueBrief_13.pdf)

Livne, E. 2015. *Violence Against Women in India: Origins, Perpetuation, and Reform*. Retrieved February 6, 2020 (https://pdfs.semanticscholar.org/136a/8beb91651c0dcb6209150820f297d216fcbd.pdf?_ga=2.25365501.1583033623.1580979208-502294903.1580979208)

Manasseh, E.L. 2007. "Women & Violence." Pp. 189–204 in *Side by Side: Gender from a Christian Perspective*, edited by B. Wood. Bangalore, India: SAIACS Press.

Mondol, R. 2014. "Ending Violence Against Women: What Can the Church Do?" Pp. 9–11 in *Drishkitone: Violence Against Women*. New Delhi: EFICOR.

---. 2017. "Not Conforming to the Social Pattern." Pp. 157–164 in *How I Changed my Mind about Women in Leadership: 20+ Indian Leaders Speak*, edited by B. Wood. Bangalore, India: SAIACS Press.

National Crime Records Bureau. 2016. *Crime in India 2016: Statistics*. New Delhi, India: Ministry of Home Affairs.

Nayak. S. 2017. "Am I Acting Against the Bible?" Pp. 177–184 in *How I Changed my Mind about Women in Leadership: 20+ Indian Leaders Speak*, edited by B. Wood. Bangalore, India: SAIACS Press. (http://ncrb.gov.in/StatPublications/CII/CII2016/pdfs/NEWPDFs/Crime%20in%20India%20-%202016%20Complete%20PDF%20291117.pdf)

Nengzakhup, S. 2017. "I Just was not Bothered about Women." Pp. 185–192 in *Side by Side: Gender from a Christian Perspective*, edited by B. Wood. Bangalore, India: SAIACS Press.

Nigam, C. 2017. "21 Lives Lost to Dowry Every Day Across India; Conviction Rate Less Than 35 Per Cent." Retrieved February 6, 2020 (http://indiatoday.intoday.in/story/dowry-deaths-national-crime-records-bureau-conviction-rate/1/935341.html)

Pal, S. 2016. "The Statistics of Gender Bias." Retrieved February 6, 2020 (http://www.thehindu.com/opinion/op-ed/the-statistics-of-gender-bias/article5827135.ece)

Pushpa Lalitha, E. 2017. "Women's Leadership in the Church of South India." *Feminist Theology*. 26(1): 80–89.

Reiher, P. 2016. "Paul and Women." Pp. 39–54 in *Women & Men: One in Christ, CBE National Conference "Better Together 2017"*, edited by D. Cooper-Clarke & K. Giles. Melbourne, Australia: Christians for Biblical Equality.

Ross, C. 2011. "Is Christianity Good for Women? A Response to Peter Lineham." *Reconsidering Gender: Evangelical Perspectives*, edited by M. Habets & B. Wood. Eugene, OR: Pickwick Publications.

Saysell, C. 2017. "Gen 1–3." *Women and Ministry in the Church: Resource for the Baptist Churches of New Zealand*, edited by C. Saysell, S. Harris, S. & E. Rice. Retrieved February 6, 2020 (http://www.lifelonglearning.nz/images/Documents/Exegesis-of-Women-and-Ministry-in-the-Church.pdf)

Shah, A. 2017. "The Delhi Gang Rape: Justice Does Not Stop at the Death Penalty." Retrieved February 6, 2020 (https://thewire.in/135919/delhi-gang-rape-death-penalty/)

Sharma, S. 2016. "Achieving Gender Equality in India: What Works, And What Doesn't." Retrieved February 6, 2020 (https://www.huffingtonpost.com/the-conversation-global/achieving-gender-equality_b_12871168.html)

Thomas Routers Foundation. 2018. "Thomas Routers Foundation Annual Poll: The World's Most Dangerous Countries for Women." Retrieved February 6, 2020 (https://poll2018.trust.org)

Udwin, L. 2015a. "Delhi Rapist Says Victim Shouldn't Have Fought Back." Retrieved February 6, 2020 (http://www.bbc.com/news/magazine-31698154)

---. (Producer & Director). 2015b. "India's Daughter" [Motion picture]. United Kingdom: Assassin Films.

United Nations Development Programme. 2016. *Human Development Report 2016: Development for Everyone*. New York, NY: United Nations Development Programme.

Vadalia, A. 2013. "The Patriarchal Indian Culture." Retrieved February 6, 2020 (http://foreignaffairsreview.co.uk/2013/11/the-patriarchal-indian-culture/)

Varghese, J. & Jacob, J. 2017. "The Goal is to Foster One Another's Gifts." Pp. 105–114 in *How I Changed my Mind about Women in Leadership: 20+ Indian Leaders Speak*, edited by B. Wood. Bangalore, India: SAIACS Press.

Varghese, T. 2013. *Abuse of Women in Christian Families: Roles of Clergymen, Church and Theological Institutions*. Delhi, India: ISPCK.

Varkey, A. 2014. "The Rights of Women in Our Context." Pp. 7–8 in *Drishkitone: Violence Against*

Women, edited by EFICOR.

Wapanginla, SCM. n.d. "A Reflection on the Situation of Women in the North East Region of India." Retrieved February 6, 2020 (http://www.wscfap.org/resources/womenspace/2003/2003-reflection_india.html)

Wood, B. 2007. "Prologue: Why a Conference Called Side by Side?" Pp. 13–18 in *Side by Side: Gender from a Christian Perspective*, edited by B. Wood. Bangalore, India: SAIACS Press.

World Economic Forum. 2018. *The Global Gender Gap Report*. Retrieved February 6, 2020 (http://www3.weforum.org/docs/WEF_GGGR_2018.pdf)

THE CASE FOR ADVOCACY IN THE STYLE OF THE BIBLICAL PROPHETS

Clinton Bergsma

> *"This ... is about some of the most disturbing people*
> *who have ever lived ..."*
> ~ Abraham Heschel (1962:vii)

INTRODUCTION

The concept of a rights-based approach to community development is at first glance a relatively new phenomenon that has arisen out of the Universal Declaration of Human Rights (UDHR). Much advocacy work of Christian communities and Christian NGOs makes reference to particular articles of the UDHR and build their cases for change from there; it is, after all, the almost globally accepted standard for the treatment of humans by humans. However, the Universal Declaration of Human Rights (UDHR) has also had significant critiques levelled at it. Some argue that it is yet another case of Western imposition (see Lorenzen, 2000:50, 57), others point to its non-binding, individualistic and litigious nature (see McIlroy, 2014), and it appears that the UDHR is often only supported when it aligns with a particular country's dominant preferences and ignored when it doesn't—such as the case with Australia's treatment of asylum seekers.

While I do not wish to argue that churches and Christian NGOs should ignore or pass over the UDHR, I would argue that some caution is needed when developing advocacy models and campaigns solely along the human rights goals and articles of the UDHR. While the UDHR deserves commendation for its attempt to set a standard for the right treatment of people, it has borrowed heavily from the Christian tradition while attempting to avoid Christianity's underpinning theological framework (see Ramachandra, 2008). Founding advocacy models on the UDHR risks losing the broad vision of *shalom* that so importantly guides the Christian tradition while leaving room for contextual expressions.

I propose that the biblical prophetic tradition is in fact a very old and tried model of a rights-based approach to achieving *shalom*, and that it offers a visionary way of rethinking our approach to the task of advocacy and human rights. I will highlight a number of major themes in the prophetic tradition[1] before considering how they might reshape the approach of churches and Christian NGOs to human rights.

What Was and Is the Prophetic Task?

The role of the prophet in the biblical narrative was primarily to proclaim the will of God (see Miller, 1987:23f). The prophet had various methods of ascertaining the will of God that included visions (2 Sam. 7:17), hearing directly from God (1 Kings 18:1), prayerful reflection (Jer. 1:11), and the use of the "urim" and "thummim" (Deut. 33:8). However, the prophetic task went beyond simply divining the present will of God, for the present will of God is always reflective of God's larger goals and future plans (LaSor

---

1   For the sake of brevity, all references to the "prophetic tradition" will be referring to the prophetic tradition in the biblical canon. This is not because I believe the prophetic tradition ended with the closing of the canon, but because the biblical prophetic tradition is the focus of this paper.

et al., 1996:229). Thus biblical prophecy at times included *fore-telling*, giving knowledge about a related future event (e.g. Jer. 16:14f) and *forth-telling*; highlighting the future consequences of a present action (e.g. Isa. 13) (LaSor et al., 199:222). The goal of fore-telling and forth-telling by the prophets was to provide guidance as to how the people of God should act in the present (LaSor et al., 1996: 229).

If the prophetic task broadly involved telling people the will of God for the present in light of the future, it is interesting how the evangelical tradition has typically understood prophecy. Pentecostalism has largely understood prophecy along fore-telling lines—the disclosure of future events—while conservatives have long held that the gift of prophecy (as fore-telling) ceased with the closing of the canon (see Grudem, 1994:1049ff), arguing that the contemporary prophetic task is primarily exegetical teaching (Grudem, 1994:630). However, in recent decades there has been a movement among evangelicals, spearheaded by the likes of Yoder, Wink and Brueggemann, to recover a prophetic task more aligned with the original role of prophet as presented in the biblical narrative. Yoder, Wink and Brueggemann argue from various angles that the message and methods of Jesus and the prophets offer a model for addressing situations of systemic injustice that does not replace one oppressive regime with another (see Yoder, 1994; Wink, 1992; Brueggemann, 2001).

OBJECTIONS TO DRAWING RIGHTS AND ADVOCACY MODELS FROM THE BIBLICAL PROPHETS

A bevy of objections may be quickly levelled at grounding an advocacy or rights approach in the biblical prophetic tradition: many consider the prophetic writings to be heavily edited and the tradition varied widely over a very long period and virtually died out in the post-exilic period (see Reddit, 2012:600). The minimal narrative data in the prophetic literature makes establishing prophetic intent a difficult task in some situations and impossible in others (Branick, 2012:294). Others argue that it is anachronistic to draw advocacy models from the prophetic tradition (see

Irwin, 2012:719, 724) and some point out the risk of "…drifting into self-confirming mirrors of our positions" (Branick, 2012:19). Some would also argue that it is inappropriate and ineffective to use theological arguments or religious practices in the secular global north, while another objection I have often encountered in the Australian context is that the task of the Church is to only "preach Christ and him crucified" (1 Cor. 1:23).

These critiques deserve consideration, and lend a helpful caution as we approach the prophetic literature and the stories of Jesus; there is—like every other time *any* portion of scripture is approached—a significant risk of reading in its pages only what we want to hear; that is an age-old issue that surfaced even in Jesus' time (c.f. Matt. 23), and is not an issue particular to the prophetic writings. The prophets' remarkably consistent message through a variety of contexts, over a number of centuries (Schmidt, 1995:579) only points to their contextual flexibility and (perhaps) the necessity of having a prophetic voice in every age. While our engagement with a secular society on the issue of rights may not get much traction with a simplistic "thus saith the LORD", to argue that Christian theology has nothing to offer a secular society empties the gospel of its worth. Lastly, to argue that the Church should stay out of political issues, and only "preach Christ and him crucified" denies the fact that the crucifixion of Jesus was—like all crucifixions circa. 30 A.D.—a political stunt intended to foster acquiescence to the Roman empire (see Wink,1992:129; Stassen, 2003: 138f). The good news of Jesus necessarily impacts all areas of life—there is nothing left untouched; by definition this must include social structures and political realms, and so the Christian community must consider what "good news" means for those areas and act on those considerations.

I would argue that perhaps our concerns with drawing from the prophetic tradition is grounded in our culturally appropriated aversion to dissenting voices—even when it is our own consciences raising the objections. Like airport sniffer dogs, we've been culturally trained to sit quietly and let our handlers sort it out when we smell something dodgy in the crowd. Yet interestingly we use "micro" subversion and resistance in day-to-day situations of inequality (see Turiel, 2003:116). For example, public bus drivers in Perth will almost always allow people a free ride if they have no money despite driving under a sign clearly stating the opposite, or the parent who permits his/her child to break what he/she considers to be an unfair household rule when the other parent is absent. These types of situations are perhaps an indication of the suppressed prophet within and our inherent ability and desire to confront injustice creatively.

JESUS THE GUIDE

Given that the prophet's role was to reveal the will of God for the present in light of the future, Jesus as *Emmanuel* is the prophet par excellence—the guiding lens through which all other biblical prophets are to be understood. Where the Old Testament prophets speak or act in ways that are seemingly contradicting Jesus, his words and actions should be given priority (e.g. Ezek. 16:37–38; c.f. Matt. 18:21–22). This does not mean that a shortcut in the search for a prophetic methodology can be made by restricting our search to the Gospels, for Jesus Himself explained his prophetic role by referring to the life and experiences of the earlier prophets (Matt. 13:13–15; Luke 4:18–21, 24). We must search the prophetic literature and the Gospels to get the clearest understanding of prophetic methodology in the Scriptures, reading the Old Testament prophets who repeatedly set the scene (and task) for the arrival of *Emmanuel* the prophet par excellence. The life of Jesus in turn assists us when we read the earlier prophets by giving us a clearer understanding of the vision God gave in the Old Testament. For these reasons I will draw from the prophets and the life of Jesus, giving Jesus greater priority and weight as I highlight a number of key themes in biblical prophetic methodology.

THE ADVOCACY METHODOLOGY OF THE BIBLICAL PROPHETS

Stripping the Gloss, Telling the Truth

Perhaps one of the most important aspects of the biblical prophets' work was their ability to shake people from their stupor and help them see things as they really are. They were like the child who stopped the regal parade by pointing out that the emperor was in fact wearing no clothes. "The prophets' ear," writes Heschel, "perceives the silent sigh ... her words begin to burn where conscience ends" (1962:9–10).

Indeed, the prophets had the rare ability to see things with a clarity the masses didn't enjoy (Wink, 1992:89). The prophets saw a lump of wood when others could only see powerful gods (Hos. 4:12; Isa. 44:14ff); they could see past the flimsy nature of expensive rituals (Amos 4; Jer. 7; Matt. 6:2; Jemielity, 1991:38) and the fragility of powerful elites (Luke 12:13–21). The prophets had the ability to see and cure those blinded by hypocrisy (2 Sam. 12:1–15; Isa. 29:13–14; Matt. 23), "wrenching consciences from a state of suspended animation" (Heschel, 1962:7). It is no wonder that the prophets were often called "seers", for they were able to perceive situations with a clarity that the majority couldn't.

Without the prophets' clarifying deconstruction of the system, there was no hope or possibility of ever changing it. Until the prophet arrived with her simplicity of vision, things just *were*. They were unchangeable, unchallengeable, set in stone for perpetuity. The voice and actions of the prophet animated the scene, liquefying what was thought to be concrete, bringing into vision things unseeable, creating space for hope of change.

But stripping the gloss necessarily entails grief and confusion (Brueggemann, 1986:32ff). The prophet must first rub mud in the eyes of the blind before the blind are able to see—and once is rarely enough. Prophetic truth-telling is painful, difficult and risky work, for there are many vested powers (human and spiritual) who have strong reasons for wanting things to remain as they are (Wink, 1992:65ff). And it is not just the powerful who wish to maintain the status quo; the oppressed are often so conditioned to be comfortable with current levels of injustice that they too don't want change (see Jost, 2015:610, 622; Goudzwaard et al., 2007:170). But the prophets did not just bring grief; their role was not to simply confront, critique and then retreat. The prophets always first caused grief because grieving for the present is a necessary precursor to desiring change for the future. As Branick states:

For the prophets the darkness of the abyss was not that of...
despair, but rather that of the obscurity of a reality beyond
human reach (2012:26).

Looking Backwards, Looking Forward

While the prophets' message was always for the present, it necessarily
encapsulated the past and the future (Hayes, 2012:603f; Heschel, 1962:12).
Hosea gave a blistering assessment of Israel's infidelity of relationship with
Yahweh and did not hold back in laying out its devastating consequences
(2:9–13). Yet the prophet's words were interspersed with reminders of
Yahweh's loving and generous provision in the past:

> She did not know
> that it was I
> who gave her
> the grain, the wine, and the oil,
> and who lavished upon her silver
> and gold that they used for Baal (2:8).

It was also interlaced with promises for the future:

> Therefore, I will now allure her,
> and bring her into the wilderness,
> and speak tenderly to her.
> From there I will give her [back] her vineyards,
> and make the Valley of Achor a door of hope (2:14–15a).

Thus the prophets' message entails pointing to the past and to
the future as a means of liberating the present. Having opened the eyes
of the audience to the deep lack of the present, the prophet must now
proceed to paint an alternative reality so that people might have hope for
a situation that turned from sweet to bitter as the prophet's words went
on (Brueggemann, 1986:97). While Brueggemann emphasises the task of
painting an alternative *future* reality in *Prophetic Imagination*, I would argue

that the looking back is also a very important aspect of the hope-imbibing process and consistent with the biblical prophetic tradition (Matthews, 2012:627; Jemielity, 1991:39). Looking back at glimpses of Eden, Egypt and Canaan added significant weight to the possibility of a new future orientation: while the goal was never to try to return to a golden era (for it birthed the present crisis), there were significant moments—glimpses of heaven—in times past that evidenced the possibility of an alternative future that supersedes even the best parts of human history (e.g. Is. 19:18f).

The future vision that the prophet provides is typically metaphoric and utopian (e.g. Is. 11:6–9), and rightly so, for it is intended to be just that—visional. To map out a clear path from the present to the future was not only impossible given the current social structures; it was also highly undesirable.[2] Some would level the charge that this type of vision is no vision at all if it is not achievable; but the prophets never for a moment suggested their vision is not achievable—the barrier that made it currently unachievable was the hearers' collective, deeply held perception that the current paradigm was unchangeable.[3] Brueggemann writes:

> [Prophets] have no advice to give people. They only want people to see differently, to re-vision life. They are not coercive. They only try to stimulate, surprise, hint, and give nuance, not more. They cannot do more, because they are making available a

---

2   It is undesirable because of its significant risks: hijacking by the powerful, the stifling of creative expressions, moving towards a mechanistic view of life and away from a relational view, and over-simplification of the dynamic, inter-related and varied nature of life. This is one of the key weaknesses of the UDHR; it is too prescriptive and not nearly visional enough. I would suggest that Martin Luther King's "I have a dream" is a much better alternative.

3   For example, the Australian population largely supports the concept of redemptive violence and cannot fathom or attempt an alternative despite redemptive violence's continual failing to bring real peace—never before in history has humanity had the ability to destroy the entire earth. And so weapons technology has infinitely increased our level of risk while draining huge amounts of money under the guise of making the world safer. The collective Australian Christian voice is largely silent on this issue, and often supportive of the current use of violence under the more palatable title of "Defence". The issue is not the vision; peace without violence is possible. The issue is the collective hearers' belief (and practice) that the present violent order is the only option available.

world that does not yet exist beyond [peoples'] imagination... (1986:24).

The biblical prophets recalled previous glimpses of *shalom* to point to the possibility of an alternative future so that their audience might begin working towards that future reality in the here and now.

With Creativity

To effectively achieve truth-telling and past-future visioning without being immediately killed, the biblical prophets needed to deliver their message in highly creative and subversive ways (see Hrynkow, 2009:113). The biblical prophets repeatedly made their point by causing such strange scenes that those nearby could not help but watch and listen, unsure as to whether they were witnessing the raving of a madman or hearing the very words of God (1 Sam. 10:9f; 19:18–24; 2 Ki. 9:1–13; Mt. 11:19).

And so the prophets held their audiences captive and helped them to see and consider the impossible by doing dramatic things (Jemielity, 1991:44f) like eating scrolls, refusing to talk, cooking over human excrement, lying down for more than a year, refusing to mourn the death of a beloved (all Ezekiel), wandering naked for three years (Isaiah), marrying the most promiscuous woman in town (Hosea), refusing to wash underwear and wearing a cattle yoke (Jeremiah), scribbling in the dirt, washing people's feet, eating with social outcasts and embracing the highly infectious (Jesus). And the prophets' words matched their strange theatrics, using poetry, comedy, metaphors, stories of hidden treasure, four-headed beasts and flying wheels to help their audiences see and think things they hadn't been able to before.

The importance of the prophetic tradition's varied and creative methods of getting their message across to a potentially hostile audience is worth reflecting on. While it was certainly the safest way to deliver such a dangerous and subversive message, the use of the arts was also perhaps the only way that the prophets could express the future things they envisioned; for they spoke of things unseen and at times almost unexplainable (see

Heschel, 1962:175f). It is significant that almost every time Jesus described the kingdom of God, he told stories and parables that gave some indication of what it is like without marking out the exact parameters. The prophetic vision is *something* like mustard seed; it is *something* like this woman's faith, that fig tree, that feast, this grape vine, those children. This cemented the *possibility* of the currently perceived to be *impossible*, for tastes and hints and glimmers of the future were present not just in the past (as argued above), but in everyday life (Matthews, 2012:629f, 633). Suddenly, pruning grapevines, having dinner parties and baking bread become activities of theological reflection and eschatological hope. The strangely captivating, other-wordly message of the prophets remains seared in the mind long after they have left.

And so the prophets perpetually balanced on a very thin wedge (Matthews, 2012:633; Heschel, 1962:19). They used highly provocative symbolism, drama, language and stories to engage their audiences, walking a tightrope between being written off as crazy and being killed off for being too provocative. It was in that tensioned space, however, that there was the possibility of people considering something entirely new, something not of the current world order.

With Love

The deep ache in the prophet's heart to have people see through the facades of the current *lo-shalom* system to an alternative future means that the prophetic heart must be deeply pastoral. While the prophets might have been some of the most cynical people around, they may well have also been some of the most *loving* people around; for the end goal of the prophet was always restoration, never condemnation (see Boda, 2012:664f). "The words of the prophet are stern, sour and stinging," wrote Heschel, "but behind the austerity is love and compassion for humanity" (1962:12).

And so the biblical prophets regularly cried tears of concern for the very people they railed against (e.g. Is. 22:4; Jer. 9:1, 13:17; Ez. 27; Lam. 3:40–50). The prophets raved and ranted, begged and pleaded with their audiences in hopes that a collective change of heart might begin to crumble the present order. This deep concern for the very soul of humanity extended even towards the ruling powers who threatened the very existence of the prophet (Brueggemann, 1986:16):

> Jerusalem, Jerusalem, the city that kills the prophets and stones those who are sent to it! How often have I desired to gather your children together as a hen gathers her brood under her wings, and you were not willing! (Lk. 13:34, ESV)

These are the words of Jesus the prophet, but they are also words of a pastor deeply concerned for the audience he was sent to minister to (Brueggemann, 1986:12). The prophet cannot but love fiercely, for to attempt the prophetic task without love sends prophets in only one direction: running Jonah-like into the belly of an ocean storm begging for an early death (c.f. Jon. 1:1–3, 4:1–4). It is not only motivationally impossible for the prophetic task to be undertaken without love, it is intrinsically impossible, for love and the kingdom of God are inextricably linked (Mt. 22:37–40; Mott, 1982:61f). The prophet cannot deconstruct the present facades without the eyes of love, and the prophet cannot see God's future clearly without the eyes of love. Indeed, the prophet's message —the prophet herself—is nothing without love (1 Cor. 13). The prophet who speaks and acts without love is nothing more than a new oppressor masquerading as a messiah (see Wink, 1992:195).

Conversely, the prophet who loves deeply and boldly does not just speak God's will; that prophet *is* God's will personified; *God's kingdom come, his will being done on earth as it is in heaven*—if only for that brief moment, a glimpse of the future in the present. A loving posture is where the prophet's power lies, for the power of love has a profound impact when it is directed against oppressors and those who are doing their bidding (see Hrynkow, 2009:114; Wink, 1992:263ff). It is here—with the vision and practice of love—that human rights has the possibility to rise above its current format (Mott, 1982:64). The prophetic task is only possible with a deep ache for the redemption of all people—including oppressors and powerful elites.

Driven by Hope, Not Effectiveness

Given all of the above—the creativity, courage and love that the prophets required in the face of a high degree of opposition from their audiences—the prophets had a low chance of getting their message across and a high chance of an early death. Jeremiah failed to convince his people not to rebel against Babylon. His scrolls were burnt by the king in a show of defiance, he had a bounty on his head at one point and was twice threatened with death. Ultimately, he failed to save Jerusalem from the destruction he so passionately warned her against. It's no wonder that Jeremiah cursed the day of his birth and is known as a prophet of lament. "Perplexity is not an alien feeling for the prophet" wrote Heschel (1962:182). The prophets were often confused, questioning themselves, their role, their capability and the God who sent them (e.g. Jer. 12:1–4; Hab. 1–2:1; Mt. 26:39, 27:46). But perplexity was not the only feeling familiar to the prophets, for the prophets were also "profound poets of hope" (Brueggemann, 1986:29).

It was a profound *hope* in the truth of their message rather than a belief in its effectiveness that sustained the prophets through their prolonged bouts of disillusion. This hope is not to be confused with optimism, for optimism can only provide energy while the path is still visible, where there is still a statistical chance of the desired outcome being achieved. Prophetic hope must cling to the very (often hidden) future it seeks to convince its audience of, embodying the message even when the walls of Jerusalem come crashing down around it. Hope carries the prophet beyond the ruins of Jerusalem because the prophetic vision reminds the prophet that the coming of the kingdom of God was never dependent on the walls of Jerusalem staying intact, or Caesar being overthrown, or the UN being a success.

This hopefulness does not mean that the prophets were unconcerned about the effectiveness of their work. The regular changing of tactics, drama and metaphors by the prophets (think Ezekiel!) is indicative of their tenacious attempts at bringing an effective message. But it was their profound hope and trust in the vision they shared that sustained them.

Thus the biblical prophets, although speaking through an incredibly wide range of space, time and methodologies held much in common with one another. Each unmasked the pretences of their time, helping people to see through the façade of current systems. Drawing from glimpses of God's kingdom in the past, they used all sorts of creative means to help their audiences imagine something not yet possible. They did this boldly, bringing their message with a deep love for the very people they railed against, hoping—always hoping, whatever the outcome—that some might be captured by the vision and attempt to bring the present order a little closer to that future reality when God's kingdom will be fully realised.

THE PROPHETS, THE CHURCH AND THE NGO

Carrying Forward the Tradition

The role of the church is to carry this prophetic tradition forward, "to be the people of a transforming story" who regularly "reassess the eschatological horizon" so that we can adjust our actions in the here and now (Barrow, 2002:208). Dominant models of advocacy often seem to be battles for power: get as many voters to send a generic email to their MP, and perhaps you will be able to force the government to change unjust legislation. This model only works however, when popular opinion swings in the desired direction, and can easily be repealed when the fickle tide of opinion changes. It also fails to address fundamental unjust patterns of thought and behaviour in the everyday punter.

Perhaps a more prophetic-centred approach would see the Church become bolder (and more creative!) in its critique of the society in which it dwells. In the Australian context, the Church is, for the most part acquiescent to and supportive of the dominant culture despite the many injustices and inequalities it perpetuates. We are not renowned for speaking Amos-like against the opulence of our times; we are not known for speaking Jesus-like against the myth of redemptive violence. We are silent when the aid budget is decreased, and silent (supportive even!) when the military budget increases. We do not seem eager to uncover the hidden gods of our culture, nor able to demarcate its oppressive regimes.

Perhaps we struggle to be prophetic *truth-tellers* because we do not have a prophetic *vision* to guide us. We do not typically offer an alternative narrative or possibility to the current order, despite a picture of hope being needed that ties past glimpses of glory to a future vision that can be seen and experienced in small, everyday ways in the present. Perhaps we struggle to have a worthy prophetic vision because we've forgotten how to *dream*, suppressing our *creativity* and reducing the arts from purveyors of the unthinkable to mere forms of entertainment. Perhaps that's because we've fixated on effectiveness and lost the courageous, powerful skills of *hope* and *love*. But perhaps my analysis is similarly of a mechanistic frame, and I'm caught in the loop of my own critique (i.e. "if we just did a, b and c, injustice would disappear").

Regardless, the Australian Church needs to recover its prophetic role, as do (broadly speaking) Australian Christian NGOs, and not just only in their advocacy work. This will necessarily mean deconstructing and critiquing our current modes of operation, rather than assuming that things just *are*. It will mean seeking out artists and prophets to help us *shalom*-shape our organisational relationships, donor interactions and campaigns against injustice. It means a willingness to try new, bold and perhaps strange (fun!) things. It might swing our gaze from this year's fundraising target to Eden and the New Jerusalem; our actions—like our vision—may become utopian and seemingly impossible, pointless to those who can't see past the current paradigms, but we *will* have vision that helps us see through our current facades to God's future reality. It will expect a tough audience (and be self-critical when there isn't one) but *love* that audience with a tenacity that seeks to win them over. I would argue this is all-important advocacy work—though it would not generally be considered such—for it advocates for change of the many structures that perpetuate the very injustices we hope to undo.

The Church and the Christian NGO cannot claim to be the people of God while attempting to dodge the prophetic role (Wright, 2010:86ff). To avoid the prophetic task is to "'tithe our mint and dill while neglecting the weightier matters"; to do so is to believe that the mantra "the temple of the Lord, the temple of the Lord, the temple of the Lord" will save us; to do so is to "build extra barns for our bounty and die that very night".

CONTEMPORARY CHALLENGES

While the prophetic task of the church and the Christian NGO is not negotiable and would do well to be shaped along the prophetic tradition in the biblical witness, it is no easy task nor a one-off event. There are many significant challenges that Australian Churches and Christian NGOs face in taking up this important work, and I wish to highlight a few in hopes they can be considered, potentially addressed and expanded upon.

In the first place one cannot help but notice a significant contrast between the demographic of the biblical prophets and the prevailing demographic of Australian Churches and NGOs. The biblical prophets —including Jesus—came from the margins; globally, the average Australian churchgoer or NGO staffer is, like myself, in the upper echelons of the wealthy. This creates a number of challenges: it is very hard to critique dominant cultural systems from within "the belly of the beast". Further, our sense of advocacy urgency is also often directly correlated to our proximity to the people suffering injustice—if they are mistreated and we are looked after—and we rarely interact—our sense of urgency will likely be low. It is also very easy to be co-opted when we are members of the elite:

> We mostly are scribes maintaining the order of the day. We mostly are appreciated by and paid by people who like it the way it is... our language becomes descriptive, because it is better to tell what is than to trust what will be ... such a flattened tongue permits no vitality ... (Brueggemann, 1986:98).

Secondly, our advocacy impetus—and willingness to follow the prophetic example—is often inversely correlated to the proportion we benefit from the current unjust system. It is very counterintuitive to work towards the dismantling of a system that we are a primary beneficiary of, even when we acknowledge the system as unjust. This is particularly pertinent for NGOs receiving government funding (see Wood, 2009) and for Christians who believe that advocacy actions are not the realm of the Church. Australian culture does not appreciate dissenting voices, and so it is very easy for us to shut down our own consciences to maintain our preference for and position in the status quo (see Brueggemann, 1986:20ff).

Third, we have been taught from birth to use violence to achieve our goals (see Hrynkow, 2009:124ff; Wink, 1992:13ff). This includes less explicit means of violence, such as forcing parents to send their children to school through the threat of withdrawing financial support they depend on, and is reflected in our perpetually building larger prisons and warships. The use of violence to achieve our goals is diametrically opposed to the prophetic tradition, and so we need to repeatedly deconstruct our hidden violent methods in order to be effective prophets. We will struggle to protest the abuse of prisoners and asylum seekers or the use of war and the technological development of weapons, while we believe in and perpetuate the myth of redemptive violence.

Fourth, we are largely captive to the idols of our time, in particular national security, material prosperity and individualism (see Goudzwaard et al., 2007). As long as we remain captive to their hypnotic gaze, we will continue to sacrifice all sorts of precious and rare things on their altars while failing to see through their fraudulent promises. Clearly a prophetic Australian Church or NGO will need prophets of their own—we need to be keenly aware of and create space for their voices (directed at us) in our midst.

These are a few contemporary challenges that can hamper the prophetic ability of churches and Christian NGOs in Australia. However, this does not mean that the Australian Church and Christian NGOs in Australia do not have a prophetic voice at all.

OLD GOALS, NEW GOAL SKINS

I wish to conclude this paper by briefly highlighting three very different examples of ways in which the prophetic tradition is currently being continued in the Australian context. I wish to stress that these are by no means the only or best examples available, but they are examples that I am familiar enough with to believe their authenticity.

The Love Makes a Way movement began in early 2014 and initially aimed to advocate for children in Australian asylum-seeker detention centres. The name reveals the vision: the belief that love has the ability to resolve Australia's perceived refugee crisis in more compassionate ways than the current approaches. The movement is highly committed to non-violence and attempts to think strategically and creatively about its advocacy efforts. Members attempt to engage police and political staff members during protests in ways that muddle assumptions about the existing order of things while offering an alternative vision to work towards. Protest actions are backed up with collaborative work with compassionate politicians, and members typically demonstrate a lived alternative by supporting local refugees in practical ways.

Working in a different but still strongly prophetic role, TEAR Australia seeks to "inform and empower" Christians to make "biblically-shaped responses to suffering and oppressed communities". Like Love Makes a Way, TEAR has a broad, future-oriented vision that shapes its response in the present. Having a broad, future-oriented vision has meant that TEAR is able to celebrate and support anything that aligns with its vision, and so it tends to have a collaborative approach that fosters locally-shaped responses to situations of poverty and injustice—even if there's no TEAR logo in sight. It encourages and supports almost any campaigns that align with its broad vision—from child trafficking to Indigenous injustice—even when it results in no direct financial support for TEAR or its overseas partners. I would suggest this is an unusual emphasis for a Christian NGO in Australia where organisational survival is often a primary driver.

On a much smaller scale, our Christian community attempts to consider life through Bryant Myers' relational paradigm. Members are not told how to act, but are invited and challenged to consider how the good news of Jesus shapes their various relationships with God, others, self and the environment. This is done in a dialogical way, with everyone invited to contribute to the conversation. While there is significantly less control than a typical church setting, commitment is high and almost all members voluntarily live in various prophetic ways. They advocate for the marginalised and caring for their practical needs; study for jobs that will allow them to serve the under-privileged; practise generosity and hospitality beyond social norms; see their work as a way of serving their co-workers and wider community; make lifestyle choices that prioritise relationships and environmental concern over "more and better".

I have intentionally chosen these three examples to demonstrate the wide diversity of the prophetic possibilities for the Christian community (including NGOs) in Australia. These three are very different from one another—just as the prophets were; but they also share much in common—just as the prophets did. They all have a vision that is much larger and more important than their own survival; their vision allows them to be truth-tellers and seers in their particular contexts; they work towards that vision with creativity, and they are driven more by hopeful vision than pragmatic effectiveness.

CONCLUSION

I have suggested that while the UDHR can be a helpful tool for advocacy efforts by Australian Churches and Christian NGOs, we must avoid grounding our advocacy work in the UDHR articles or having them as our end goal. I have argued that the prophetic tradition in the biblical witness offers an older and better model for advocacy. It is less prescriptive, less legislative and much more visional. A prophetic approach to advocacy is fundamentally different and often admired—not easily dismissed—by its opponents. The goal of prophetic work is not to force everyone into the mould of *shalom*; for to do so would be *lo-shalom*. Rather, the prophetic task is to unmask the current paradigm so that people can realise that the idols they're worshipping are mere lumps of wood, while also providing an alternative vision that is supported by glimpses in the past and present which suggest that a different future is possible.

This is no easy task, particularly if the prophet is as broken and corrupted as the audience. The modern prophet must have a profound hope of restoration not just for the audience and powerful elites, but also a profound hope of restoration for the self. The modern prophet must embrace creativity, and not avoid fun, playfulness or the very real possibility of failure. They will continually need to re-centre their hearts on love, for they know the goal cannot be reached otherwise. They will be afraid of many things, but will be most afraid of things as they presently are, for modern prophets are drawn forward by the "impossible" future already proved true in the life of Jesus. The modern prophet does not search for the perfect formula of behavioural change or the definitive piece of legislation. The prophets yearn for *shalom* and refuse to settle on any imitations while they wait for the return of Jesus.

Perhaps Heschel was right. Christians like these will be "some of the most disturbing people who have ever lived".

REFERENCES

Barrow, S. 2002. "Circling the Square: Moving between Practical Politics and Eschatological Performance." Political Theology. 3(2): 197–215.

Boda, M.J. 2012. "Repentance." Pp. 664–671 in *Dictionary of the Old Testament Prophets*, edited by M.J. Boda and J. G. McConville. Downers Grove, IL: IVP Academic.

Branick, V.P. 2012. *Understanding the Prophets and their Books*. New York, NY: Paulist Press.

Brueggemann, W. 1986. *Hopeful Imagination: Prophetic Voices in Exile*. Philadelphia, PA: Fortress Press.

---. 2001. *The Prophetic Imagination*. 2nd ed. Minneapolis, MN: Fortress Press.

Greenspahn, F.E. 1989. "Why Prophecy Ceased." *Journal of Biblical Literature*. 108(1): 37–49.

Goudzwaard, B., M. Vander Vennen and D. Van Heemst. 2007. *Hope in Troubled Times: A New Vision for Confronting Global Crises*. Grand Rapids, MI: Baker Academic.

Hays, J.D. 2012. "Prophecy and Eschatology in Christian Theology" Pp. 601–610 in *Dictionary of the Old Testament prophets*, edited by M.J. Boda and J. G. McConville. Downers Grove, IL: IVP Academic.

Heschel, A.J. 1962. *The Prophets*, Two Volumes in One. Peabody, MA: Hendrikson Publishers.

Hrynkow, C. 2009. "Christian Peacemaker Teams, Solidarist Nonviolent Activism, and the Politics of Peace: Peace Witness that Challenges Militarism and Destructive Violence." *The Canadian Journal of Peace and Conflict Studies*. 41(1): 111–134.

Irwin, B.P. 2012. "Social Justice." Pp. 719–734 in *Dictionary of the Old Testament Prophets*, edited by M.J. Boda and J. G. McConville. Downers Grove, IL: IVP Academic.

Jemielity, T. 1991. "The Prophetic Character: Good, Heroic and Naïve." *Literature and Theology*. 5(1): 37–48.

Jost, J. 2015. "Resistance to Change: A Social Psychological Perspective." *Social Research*, 82(3): 607–636.

LaSor, W.S., D.A. Hubbard & F.W. Bush. 1996. *Old Testament Survey: The Message, Form and Background of the Old Testament*. 2nd ed. Grand Rapids, MI: William B. Eerdmans.

Lorenzen, T. 2000. "Towards a Theology of Human Rights." *Review and Expositor*. 97: 49–66.

Matthews, V.H. 2012. "Prophecy and Society." Pp. 623–633 in *Dictionary of the Old Testament Prophets*, edited by M.J. Boda and J. G. McConville. Downers Grove, IL: IVP Academic.

McIlroy, D. 2013. "The Problem of Human Rights." *Ethics in Brief*. 19(3): n.p.

Miller, J.W. 1987. *Meet the Prophets: A Beginner's Guide to the Books of the Biblical Prophets*. New York, NY: Paulist Press.

Mott, S. 1982. *Biblical Ethics and Social Change*. New York, NY: Oxford University Press.

Nepstad, S.E. 2009. "Disruptive Action and the Prophetic Tradition: War Resistance in the Plowshares Movement." *U.S. Catholic Historian*. 27(2): 97–113.

Ramachandra, V. 2008. *Subverting Global Myths: Theology and the Public Issues Shaping Our World*. Downers Grove, IL: InterVarsity Press.

Reddit, P.L. 2012. "History of prophecy." Pp. 587–601 in *Dictionary of the Old Testament Prophets*, edited by M.J. Boda and J. G. McConville. Downers Grove, IL: IVP Academic.

Schmidt, W.H. 1995. "Contemporary issues." Pp. 579–581 in *The Place is too Small for Us: The Israelite Prophets in Recent Scholarship*, edited by R.P. Gordon. Winona Lake, PA: Eisenbrauns.

Sloane, A. 2011. "Justifying Advocacy: A Biblical and Theological Rationale for Speaking the Truth to Power on Behalf of the Vulnerable." John Saunders Lecture 2011.

Stackhouse, M. 2005. "Why Human Rights Need God: A Christian Perspective." Pp. 25–40 in *Does Human Rights Need God?*, edited by E. Basnett, & B. Bucar. Grand Rapids, MI: William B. Eerdmans.

Stassen, G.H. 2003. "It is Time to Take Jesus Back: In Celebration of the Fiftieth Anniversary of H. Richard Nieburhr's "Christ and Culture"." *Journal of the Society of Christian Ethics.* 23(1): 133–143.

Turiel, E. 2003. "Resistance and Subversion in Everyday Life." *Journal of Moral Education.* 32(2): 115–130.

Wink, W. 1992. *Engaging the Powers: Discernment and Resistance in a World of Domination.* Minneapolis, MN: Fortress Press.

Wood, R.L. 2009. "Taming Prophetic Religion? Faith-based Activism and Welfare Provision." *International Journal of Public Theology.* (3): 78–95.

Wright, C. 2004. *Old Testament Ethics for the People of God.* Downers Grove, IL: InterVarsity Press.

---. 2010. *The Mission of God's people: A Biblical Theology of the Church's Mission.* Grand Rapids, MI: Zondervan.

Yoder, J.H. 1994. *The Politics of Jesus.* 2nd ed. Grand Rapids, MI: William B. Eerdmans.

LET JUSTICE ROLL:
EVOLUTION OF A RIGHTS-BASED
APPROACH TO DEVELOPMENT

UMN 2005–2020

Lyn Jackson

JUSTICE TURNS TO BITTERNESS (AMOS 5:7)

Like many low-caste community villages in Nepal, the Kumal settlement of Pipaltar, Dhading, straggles along a stony ridgeline above terraced fields that tumble down to the river far below. Above the village, the blue-grey ranks of the Pahad[1] march northwards toward the high Himals. A little below, the thatched and tin roofs of the high-caste village of Majuwa peek through between stands of bananas (see fig. 1).

Unlike that of many low-caste villages, the Kumals' land is fertile, with the potential to provide more than enough food for the villagers. When the monsoon is good, the Kumals can eat well. But when there's insufficient rain or rain at the wrong time, they go hungry.

They shouldn't. Back in 1977, an irrigation channel was built to bring water from springs in the mountains to the village. Each year, the Kumals'

---

*   Photographs by UMN's Ramesh Maharjan
1   Pahad: The "middle hills" of Nepal.

Figure 1

fields glinted as water filled their terraces, regardless of the rains. After the rice was harvested, they would plant winter wheat. Each house had its vegetable garden, and women were spared the long walk down to the river and back up with heavy brass water pots.

For three years.

Then the irrigation canal dried up, and fell into disrepair. The Kumals were again at the mercy of the weather. The Majuwa villagers had cut into the canal above the village and diverted its precious water to their own fields. The Kumals protested, but in vain. Their delegation to the Panchayat[2] office was useless—the Big People weren't interested in hearing from a ragtag group of illiterate low-caste layabouts, just looking for government handouts. Now that they were dependent on the Majuwas for work in *their* irrigated fields, no one wanted to take a stand. The Kumals settled back into poverty. Their children didn't go to school; when a Health Post was built under a government plan, it remained unstaffed, locked and empty. People scorned the Kumals as backward, dirty, ignorant and lazy.

For 30 years.

---

2   Panchayat: The local level of government at that time.

SEEING THE OPPRESSION OF THE PEOPLE (AMOS 3:9)

Poverty is easy to see; oppression less so. The tangled roots of poverty in Nepal tap deep into caste prejudices. They anchor themselves in different ethnicities and religious traditions. They are nourished by remoteness and strengthened by discrimination. So poverty thrives on oppression. It entangles thousands of Nepali communities, particularly damaging to women and girls, people with disabilities, people of low caste or different ethnicity. Its rotting fruit fertilises its growth: poor health, little education, political powerlessness, and religious fatalism.

Cut off one branch, and another sprouts; saw it off at ground level and the stump will shoot.

The United Mission to Nepal (UMN) has been addressing poverty and disadvantage in Nepal for 65 years. Health clinics grew into hospitals and community health projects. Schools were started; working with government and community schools improved the quality of teaching and learning. UMN kicked off industrial development with apprentice-training and hydropower, then community income-generation and entrepreneurship. It trained farmers in animal husbandry and improved agricultural techniques, promoted alternative crops, and championed organic pesticides and fertilisers, established marketing co-operatives and sought "value-added" food processing options. Over the years, hundreds of thousands of Nepalis have benefited from programmes designed to "serve the people of Nepal, in the Name and Spirit of Jesus Christ".[3]

But Nepal is still one of the poorest countries in Asia. A quarter of the population lives in poverty; life expectancy at birth is just over 68 years. Malnutrition stunts 41 percent of children under five. Only 57 percent of adults are literate (UNDP, 2014; World Food Program, 2014). The gap between the prosperous and the poor is growing: while the wealthy in Kathmandu live in comfort, people like the Kumals sit in the dirt and wait for the rain. Poverty is not being made history; development activities alone will not defeat it.

---

3   UMN's Mission Statement, 1977–2010. "To serve the people of Nepal, in the Name and Spirit of Jesus Christ, and to make Him known in word and deed, thus strengthening the universal Church in its total ministry."

Cut off one branch, and another sprouts; saw it off at ground level and the stump will shoot.

The Poor are Deprived of Justice (Amos 5:12)

Tackling poverty means dealing with the injustice at its roots. During the 1980s and 1990s, the development community became increasingly aware that it was "focused on the symptoms of crisis and was failing to tackle the underlying causes" (Harris-Curtis et al., 2005:9). While development agencies realised they needed to address structural and systemic causes of poverty and exclusion, human rights organisations saw that achieving rights involved more than legal frameworks and international conventions. It meant community involvement in the process, at all levels (VeneKlasen et al., 2004:1). Clearly, each approach had much to offer the other; now those two strengths needed to be combined into an integrated approach.

Marks (2003) outlines seven ways in which the practice of development can be enriched by a human rights perspective.

1. *A holistic approach.* Rights are indivisible, interdependent and in-terrelated. There should be no division in practice between civil/political rights and economic, social and cultural rights, i.e., the business of development. All are essential for human dignity. All require the transformation of institutions and practices.

2. *A rights-based approach.* Attention to human rights is integrated into a sustainable development framework, effectively ensuring that people realise their rights, rather than addressing violations legalistically. Chapman sees a rights-based approach as "an essential part of a holistic process" as it "builds on people's desire for dignity and the satisfaction of their basic needs" (2005:3, 5). This is more than just adding rights language and advocacy to development. Rather, rights and advocacy are the political/policy side of development, while development/participation are the practical side of rights and advocacy. The resulting interplay between rights and responsibilities is sometimes expressed as

moving development work from charity to justice (VeneKlasen et al., 2004:4, 11). Empowerment is a key factor, as people become "agents and subjects" rather than "objects" of their own development (IDS, 2003:2).

3. *A social justice approach.* This approach assesses "the degree to which the institutions of a social system are treating the persons and groups they affect in a morally appropriate and ... even-handed way" (Tomas Pogge, in Marks, 2003:7). It focuses on the moral imperative of eliminating social inequalities, using human rights as a set of agreed standards to define what that means. Paul Farmer uses "Observe, Judge, Act" as a process for challenging unjust structures (in Marks, 2003:7).

4. *A capabilities approach.* Characterising development in terms of human freedom, Amartya Sen brought freedoms and rights into the centre of the debate. "Capabilities" are the options available to an individual, while "functioning" refers to the exercise of those options. Poverty is the deprivation of capabilities or options. Sen proposes that public policy should focus more on capabilities, rather than functioning. Human development cannot proceed without the realisation of human rights (ODI, 2001).

5. *A "right to development" approach.* The UN Declaration on the Right to Development sees development as fundamental to the realisation of all other human rights and freedoms (1986, Article 1). This approach insists that development should not be at the expense of human rights, and that development policies and practices should be human-centred and participatory, "instruments of democratisation and the empowerment of civil society" (Marks, 2003:15).

6. *A responsibilities approach.* The focus here falls on the responsibilities of duty-bearers, primarily states. Low-income countries have a responsibility to see that everyone gets a fair share of scarce resources; wealthy countries have an obligation to help

others attain these freedoms. Individuals also have a duty to others, to help create "human rights communities" (Marks, 2003:21).

7. *A human rights education approach.* Based on the ground-breaking work of Paolo Freire, this approach aims for social transformation through the development of people's capacity to critique existing power structures. Participants learn about their rights through a process of dialogue, very different from the more usual human rights "awareness-raising" methods of simply telling people about their rights (VeneKlasen et al., 2004:32; Ife, 2010:202–203). Empowerment is the goal, transforming "beggars into claimants" (Marks, 2003:23).

These seven approaches offer different perspectives on the situation of the Kumals. Their poverty was not simply economic, but a result of a range of issues holistically affecting their lives (#1). UMN's "Life of Poverty" model is helpful in analysing the causes of their predicament.

Figure 2: UMN's "Life of Poverty" Model, 2016

The Kumals were food-insecure, **vulnerable** to ill-health and unable to access education or income opportunities. Lacking a secure water supply, they were also at risk from the changing weather and rainfall patterns resulting from **climate change.** The loss of water was **unjust,** perpetrated on them because of their powerlessness caste status, based in religious beliefs and resulting in **shame and disrespect.** Their attempts at redress led to conflict with the neighbouring village, and their failure led to **hopelessness and despair.** This in turn resulted in alcohol abuse and sexual/domestic violence, quarrels between neighbours and alienation of youth—more conflict in an already stressed community.

The Kumals' situation was one of social injustice (#3)—while other villages were receiving some benefits of development, the Kumals were losing what little they had. As a result, the Kumals were deprived of their opportunities to choose (capabilities) and live (functioning) with dignity and freedom (#4). In this situation, marrying participatory development practices with a rights-based approach (#2) made good sense. Dealing with the water problem in isolation would leave many other issues unresolved and, given the enmity between the two villages and lack of support from the district administration, might not be sustainable anyway. The Kumals' right to development needed to be realised (#5) in order for all these issues to be addressed, though they had limited awareness, and no tools to do much about it. They themselves needed to be able to question the caste barriers which excluded them (#7), and break through the fatalism and despair which overwhelmed them. In addition, the duty-bearers (in this case, the district administrators) needed to be challenged to fulfil their responsibilities (#6), preferably by the Kumals themselves.

These are all compelling reasons to work with the Kumals, not just to address the surface issues of food insecurity, ill-health and material poverty, but to develop their capacity to challenge oppressive structures and realise their rights. For UMN as a Christian organisation, another more fundamental imperative urges us to act on behalf of communities like this: the biblical injunction to "let justice roll on like a river, and righteousness like a never-failing stream" (Amos 5:24, NIV).

HATE EVIL, LOVE GOOD, MAINTAIN JUSTICE (AMOS 5:15)

A Christian understanding of human rights and justice begins at the beginning—with human beings, male and female, made in the image of God, formed *complete and for a purpose* (#1). Each individual's worth is embedded in this understanding of human beings as sacred. "When we stand before another person, however destitute, disabled, diseased or degraded, we stand before something which is the vehicle of the divine" (Ramachandra, 2008:7, 15). Some things should never be done to them; some things ought to be done for them (Stackhouse, 2005:37). God created human beings to have choices, to have the capability to live in the created world and fulfil the task of caring for creation; depriving people of capabilities (#4) is contrary to God's design. An attack on an image-bearer of God is an attack on God himself (Roy, 2009:6; Prov. 14:31). In contrast, "the observance of human rights brings glory and honour to God, for God imparts divine glory to humankind with the *imago Dei*" (Marshall, 2001:63). When we look at the Kumals, we see our joint humanity, our shared Parenthood, as whole people whose whole lives matter to God.

Human rights emerge from "key strands of Biblically rooted religions" (Stackhouse, 2005:33), and reflect the desire that all people should enjoy the minimum conditions and freedoms that make life possible. Marshall (2001:72) describes the Decalogue as "Israel's Bill of Rights", and goes on to show how human rights are evident throughout the Scriptures, in Creation, Covenant, Incarnation, Church and the coming Kingdom. Lorenzen comments that "human rights are there to curb selfishness, ruthlessness and injustice, to protect the interests of the vulnerable, weak and oppressed", and points out that "this is God's business" (Lorenzen, 2000:6). In taking up a *rights-based approach* (#2), Christian organisations like UMN are aligning with Biblical principles. Williams' observation of how this works is very applicable to the situation of the Kumals, "The shared acknowledgement of human rights is the common practice of scrutinising what is going on with an eye to who is being left out and how they might be integrated better into the common activity of the community" (2012:9).

The *social justice approach* (#3) is an excellent fit with Christian organisations that take God's requirement for his people to seek justice. The Israelites were to be a blessing to the nations, "shaped by [God's] own ethical character, with specific attention to righteousness and justice in a world filled with oppression and injustice" (Wright, 2010:94). Today, Christians are called to "follow the way of the Lord" (Wright, 2010). God's justice is restorative (Roy, 2009:14); it demands that wrongs be righted, and that people who are oppressed enjoy redress (Mott, 1982:61). Stassen calls for "the kind of justice Jesus cares about"—putting limits on dominance and power, confronting the wealthy and those who dominate others, seeing that the outcasts are included (Stassen, 2006:168). The Kumals needed people who, following God's example, would put themselves on the side of the poor and see that justice was done.

The *right to development* (#5) is not only the right to life, but to a certain quality of life (Marshall, 2001:75). Old Testament law provided for the poor, but was also designed to ensure that poverty, if experienced, was a temporary condition; Sabbath and Jubilee laws required the cancellation of debt, the freeing of slaves and the return of land to its original holders (Lev. 25). Means of production could not be taken as collateral for loans (Deut. 24:6). Development and prosperity was to be a communal good, contributing to Shalom, shared by all (Padilla, 2009:190; Williams, 2012:6). As a Christian development agency, UMN champions a process of development that values human dignity and leads people towards "fullness of life"[4] —*all* people, particularly those most disadvantaged, like the Kumals.

The Bible has a lot to say about *responsibilities* (#6). Israelite rulers were to be different from the kings of neighbouring countries. Rather than exploit ordinary people for their own gain, they were to be just and righteous, adhering to God's standards (Ps. 72; 82). The duty of the king as the most powerful was to champion the cause of the least powerful (Wright, 2004:272; Marshall, 2001:84). Power and authority were gifts given to a community through a person of power for those without it (Sloane, 2011:5). Modern rulers, whether hereditary or democratically elected, are not exempt from this requirement. Psalm 82 depicts God's frustration with the "gods" of this earth. He calls on them to "defend the cause of the weak and fatherless; maintain the rights of the poor and oppressed. Rescue the weak and needy; deliver them from the hand of the wicked" (Ps. 82:3–4, NIV 1984).

But while kings of Israel were especially tasked to see that justice was done, responsibility lay with the whole community (Roy, 2009:25). Marshall suggests that "human rights may be thought of as the rights each person has to have other persons fulfill their responsibility to God with regard to him or her" (2001:57). In the case of the Kumals, UMN as an INGO has power, in the form of knowledge, skills, connections and strategies. These give it a voice—a "God-given gift and responsibility", which is to be used "for God's glory and in the service of the poor" (Sloane, 2011:8).

---

4   UMN Vision: "Fullness of life for all, in a transformed Nepali society", based on John 10:10. See Appendix A.

If human beings are about achieving the dignity afforded them by God, then their involvement is key to the process of getting justice. The struggle for justice is the concern of every citizen; rights are a matter of ordinary people claiming what is theirs (Ramachandra, 2008:2). Maggay suggests that we must "engage the deep structures of culture" in order to "make space for grace" (2005:89, 91), while Wieland talks about "unmasking unjust social systems in order to transform them" (2002:17).

In a rights education approach (#7), the agency of people to be part of the process is critical: our challenge as Christian development workers is "how to make them [the poor, in this case the Kumals] and ourselves more nearly approximate to the redemptive purposes God has for the world" (Stackhouse, 2005:38).

FROM SHEPHERD TO PROPHET (AMOS 7:14–15)

2000–2010: Insurgency, Instability, and Change

Until 2000, UMN worked in Education, Health, Industrial Development and Rural Development. Apart from several large institutions (hospitals, schools) and companies (Industrial Development), work was typically large-scale community development, around an entry point aligning with the relevant department. Projects were negotiated with local and national governments, and funded, staffed and operated directly by UMN. Projects generally moved towards an empowerment approach, encouraging local ownership through advisory committees and equipping groups to develop and implement their own activities.

A Maoist insurgency raged from 1996–2006 and put externally-funded and operated development work at risk. Offices in several districts were attacked and equipment stolen; staff were threatened, kidnapped, and interrogated. Several large projects were closed, while others were suspended or downscaled. Although it was a very traumatic time, the UMN staff learnt some valuable lessons, which helped shape their future thinking.

The Dailekh Education Project[5] exemplifies this. Built around women's literacy groups, it was linked with UMN's partnership with local government schools, improving the quality of teaching and learning through teacher training and resourcing. Women from literacy groups visited their children's schools and teachers and became part of Parents' and Teachers' Associations and School Management Committees, learning what educational services their children should have been receiving. A great day it was, when a group of irate women marched into the District Education Officer's room, thumped on his desk and demanded that teachers attend school regularly, and that the long-awaited textbooks be provided—at once!

Dailekh was, however, largely under Maoist control. Community empowerment was not on their agenda. The UMN office was burned down, staff held at gunpoint, and one staff member was even dragged off into the jungle. Some village women reacted with incredible bravery, following the cadres for hours, demanding that the staff member be released. Eventually he was, but threats against the lives of staff made the project too risky to be continued.

Eight months later, a UMN staff member visiting the area found that, of the 40 women's groups, more than 30 were still operating: practicing their literacy skills with local facilitators, continuing their group savings, discussing local issues and protecting each other's interests. If community empowerment made sense where project longevity was uncertain, surely it also made sense in more peaceful times. Experience meshed with emerging development theories: building the capacity of local people and groups, helping them make service providers accountable, encouraging and supporting their participation in local government processes—these actions pointed towards more effective, long-term, sustainable ways in which poverty and injustice could be tackled.

---

5   The story of the Dailekh Education Project is drawn from a number of internal UMN reports and discussion papers, along with the author's personal recollections, as UMN Education Director during much of this time. It was checked for accuracy with the gentleman who was Project Director for Dailekh at the time.

When UMN embarked on a major restructuring process (2001–2005), the ten agreed "Strategic Directions" included *Addressing Injustice and Capacity Building*. The 2003–2008 Strategic Plan lists this goal: "UMN and its partners will be increasingly effective in advocating for justice and equality in Nepal" (UMN, 2002). By late 2005, an Advocacy unit had been created within the Technical Advisory Team as an Area of Work (Booth, 2009:32).

There were two key problems with these decisions. Firstly, the focus of advocacy had shifted from community advocacy (as in the Dailekh example) to advocacy done *by* UMN and its partners, *on behalf of* poor communities. Secondly, placing Advocacy as an Area of Work isolated it from the activities of other teams, making it the responsibility of the Advocacy team, rather than something embedded in every project. Initially the Advocacy team was small and relatively junior, with no Advocacy officers placed in "clusters".[6] Moreover, the Advocacy team was supposed to provide assistance and training across other technical areas as required; this rarely happened. UMN's energies were heavily invested in developing the organisational capacity of partners, which was very successful. Technical teams helped partners implement competent projects in health, livelihoods, education, etc. However, there is little evidence that the harder development questions were being asked: Why are the poorest communities missing out on services in health and education? Why are their livelihood opportunities so curtailed? What is cutting these communities off from the development gains others are experiencing? Why is justice not being done, and what can we, along with the communities we work with, do about it?

The mid-term review that raised these issues (UMN, 2006) reframed the strategy to include "Approaches"—including Addressing Injustice and Inequality (Booth, 2009:86). There was still little clarity on what exactly this meant in practice, who was responsible for it, and how it would fit with the technically-oriented projects being implemented by partners.

---

6   Clusters: UMN's local working areas. A "cluster" might be managing a number of different projects as well as supporting several local partner organisations.

2010–2015: First Steps in Advocacy

Planning for the 2010–2015 Strategic Plan was rigorous and wide-ranging. The document again listed Advocacy as an Approach, but laid out much clearer expectations and objectives (UMN, 2010:26–28). The language is more social-justice oriented than rights-based, but it envisaged the Advocacy team working alongside the technical teams "to speak out for and with excluded groups in order to influence policy, decisions, attitudes and behaviours of those in authority". Engagement was to be at various levels, from community empowerment to participation in international campaigns.

Plans for the technical teams also contained advocacy activities. The Education team planned to "mobilise parents and communities to be aware of education policy and participate in local education management and planning processes" (ibid.:29). A Health team objective was that "People have equitable access to good quality and sustainable health care services" (ibid.:31), and the Peacebuilding team would "promote gender equality" and "advocate for an end to harmful discrimination in all its forms" (ibid.:32).

Over the next five years, addressing human rights and poverty issues through advocacy became a much more integrated part of UMN's work. Teams began to engage more in advocacy work, and to call on the Advocacy team for assistance, while the Advocacy team itself began several projects of its own. Some examples are:

1. *Disability rights.* People with disabilities are among the most disadvantaged in Nepal, suffering cultural and religious stigma. Although the Government provides a small pension for people with disabilities, few families in rural areas are aware of this. Awareness campaigns in villages and "registration camps" provided assistance for eligible people to get disability ID cards (1448 in 2013–2014 — UMN, 2014d).

2. *Dalit rights.*[7] Similarly, several of UMN's local partners focus on Dalit communities. Apart from livelihoods, health and education activities, partners have advocated for equality for Dalits, and assisted Dalits to register cases of discrimination or harassment with the police. In 2013–2014, 22 cases were documented and referred for legal redress (UMN, 2014d).

3. *Children's and women's rights.* Women's groups and child clubs have held discussions about rights and responsibilities. Two large Child-Centred Community Development projects have been particularly influential. Similarly, an Anti-Human Trafficking Project found that focusing more broadly on women's rights was helpful in preventing the kinds of situations that made young women particularly vulnerable to trafficking.

4. *Mental Health.* UMN had been very influential in getting mental health onto the national health agenda in the 1990s. In 2012, UMN helped set up a National Mental Health Network, bringing together 20 organisations involved in mental health training, treatment and advocacy. The Network advocated for mental health to be included in the National Health Strategy, for a Mental Health contact person within the Ministry of Health, and for psychotropic drugs to be available at Health Posts for basic treatment of mental illness.

5. *Participatory Planning Process (PPP).* Although the Local Self-Governance Act legislated a very participatory process for the allocation of VDC and DDC[8] budgets, in practice, the local elites tended to make these decisions. In response, UMN developed a community engagement process to assist communities in taking up this opportunity. Over three years, they trained

---

7   Dalits: Members of the low-caste community. Discrimination on the basis of caste is technically illegal in Nepal, but is endemic in the culture.

8   DDC: District Development Committee, at the time the second layer of government in Nepal. There were 75 districts in the country. Since then, the federal structure of Nepal has changed.

317 community facilitators in 32 VDCs in ten districts with great success, receiving approval for local projects worth AUD 310,000, which were subsequently implemented.[9] The results have increased community confidence and empowerment, and levels of accountability for local officials. Women, Dalits and people with disabilities have been appointed to local committees, and continue to take an active role in local affairs.

6. *Christian Commitment to Building a New Nepal.* Churches in Nepal have slowly emerged from isolation and are seeking engagement with their communities, since Nepal was declared a secular state in 2006. UMN helped facilitate a massive consultation effort involving more than 1600 Christians in most of Nepal's 75 districts. Participants listed and prioritised what they felt were the nation's needs, and committed themselves to doing what they could to realise these. The resulting document, *Christian Commitment to Building a New Nepal*, was presented to the District Administrative Officers in all 75 districts, the Chair of the Constitutional Assembly and the Vice President of Nepal on 25 May 2011. Most Nepali Christians had never before been involved in any political activity, apart from voting (Thurley, 2011).

7. *The Pipaltar Project.*[10] The Kumals were identified as one of the neediest communities in Dhading district. Careful analysis and lengthy discussions with local people showed that the roots of the Kumals' poverty needed to be addressed. UMN's Advocacy team, together with the local partner Jagatjyothi Community Development Society (JCDS), had the opportunity to explore how advocacy could be integrated with other community

---

9   This only counts projects approved in VDCs in the year in which UMN and its partners directly supported the community. In subsequent years, communities independently participated in the process and applied for funding, many with success.

10   Information drawn from various UMN internal and donor reports, especially *UMN Advocacy Action Reflection*, January 2014.

development approaches to make substantive changes in peoples' lives.

First, the water problem. UMN worked with the Kumals, helping them prepare for meetings with district administrators. To support their efforts, local media were informed and covered the story. After many discussions and lengthy meetings, the Kumals' right to water was affirmed, and the irrigation canal reinstated.

Naturally, the Majuwas were furious. They had not only lost their water, but their labour force as well. UMN's Peacebuilding team conducted Do No Harm workshops and mediation sessions, brokering a deal to share water between the communities. Several Kumal men were trained to manage the system. Kumal families also found it helpful to have some members continue to work for the Majuwas, while others worked their own land.

The Kumals turned their attention to health services. Using the skills they had learned, and with help from UMN's partner, they argued for permanent staffing of the Health Post, and the establishment of a birthing centre. Eventually, the District Health Office appointed a Community Medical Assistant and an Auxiliary Nurse Midwife, along with Female Volunteer Health Workers provided by the community and trained by UMN. Women in particular began to enjoy the benefits of better health services. Now, almost all pregnant women have regular check-ups, deliver at the birthing centre, and receive post-natal support.

Other activities included the formation of a Child Club and three farmers' groups, scholarships to keep vulnerable students at school, and an anti-domestic-violence campaign conducted by women's group members. The farmers' groups participated in Ward-level planning meetings and developed proposals to put forward to the VDC through the Participatory Planning Process.

Things were still not perfect for the Kumals. Various community groups were fragile, and needed more capacity-building. Education facilities were still poor; farmers needed help to develop markets for their produce; the Water Users' Group had difficulty providing for maintenance costs; high incidence of early marriage continued to take teenage girls out of school. But the Kumals no longer felt helpless; they appreciated the input from UMN and wanted it to continue, but they had also felt the thrill of success through their own efforts. The government administration in Dhading was more aware of its responsibilities, and the local media played their part by keeping them accountable.

UMN harvested a great deal of knowledge from these experiences:

- The process strengthened advocacy skills across UMN, in partner organisations, and in communities. UMN published an advocacy skills manual in Nepali. The Advocacy team worked with partners and communities to develop basic skills and strategies and increase confidence—all these transferrable to new situations.

- UMN realised that although helping people tap into the existing government provisions required a great deal of effort, it paid off. This was relatively easy with disability issues, but the PPP intervention was much more complex, and required systematic, house-to-house visits to ensure the participation of marginalised groups—women, elderly people, people with disabilities, etc. Such groups needed training and confidence-building in order to effectively participate (Cornwall, 2003).

- UMN also recognised the need for collaborative effort. Staff saw the need to work together, to draw on different types of expertise, bring together local stakeholders and tap into local resources. They needed to make sure the technical teams did not end up working in "silos" (VeneKlasen et al., 2004:25). Since acquiring these insights, UMN has implemented new structures and procedures to address this problem.

- One thing will lead to another. As a community deals with one issue, others emerge. There is no perfect community, no "end-point" (Ife, 2010:230). New opportunities open up; hence the importance of transferring skills to new situations.

- Groups can be powerful agents for change, but they need careful nurturing, capacity-building and support (UMN, 2014a). Child clubs, women's groups, farmers' groups, resource management groups—they all can be important in community empowerment, but much depends on the skills of the facilitator, especially in the early stages.

- Rights need to be negotiated *between* communities as well as within them. "Community" can be a contested term (Ife, 2010:123); Pipaltar and Majuwa needed to co-exist as a wider community, sharing resources.

- Developing accountability need not be combative. Many local officials have appreciated efforts to enrol people with disabilities in the government support scheme, or encourage people to participate in the VDC budgeting process. "No service is greater than changing lives," said Chief District Officer Ananda Paudel (UMN, 2014b:29).

But above all, UMN learnt the importance of helping a community dig down to the roots of poverty and the sources of vulnerability, ease them out of the ground, and free up the soil for more productive purposes. It takes time, patience, skill, and a readiness to step back and give communities the space to do the work themselves. It requires a great deal of capacity-building, an intensive investment of effort, and a close, respectful relationship with the community.

2015–2020: Pursuing Justice

UMN's Strategic Plan 2015–2020 builds on the learning and experience of the last ten years, and propels the organisation further towards a rights-based approach to development. Key changes in strategy include:

- A clear definition of the people whose lives UMN most wishes to affect: the "poorest of the people living in poverty". The Life of Poverty diagram will help identify these people in each regional context, but every programme will need to show how its work affects key groups: women, particularly widows and deserted wives; Dalits; people with disabilities; and children and adolescents, particularly girls. UMN seeks to identify and address the barriers that keep them from enjoying "fullness of life" (UMN, 2014c: 27–28). "Fullness of life" (as defined by UMN's Fullness of Life model – Appendix B) is thus understood as a set of "rights" that people are entitled to, while overcoming the barriers is seen as pursuing justice for/with them.

- A focus on "community transformation". Community transformation is "a long-term process of continuous positive change in which people move from a life of poverty towards fullness of life". It involves:
  - building on the strengths, skills, knowledge, capacities, assets, dreams and aspirations of the poorest of the people living in poverty;

> - working towards more just and equitable power relationships;
> - achieving lasting changes in worldview, values and attitudes of all in the community;
> - breaking down or overcoming the barriers that prevent people from moving from "Life of Poverty" to "Fullness of Life" (UMN, 2014c:28).

Community transformation requires working with whole communities, not just the "poorest people living in poverty". This includes:

> - the powerful and the powerless;
> - the duty bearers and the rights holders;
> - those who are in authority and those who are not (UMN, 2014c:28).

- Two types of advocacy. The Strategic Plan endorses the importance of advocacy as a component of UMN's work, and differentiates two distinct strands of advocacy:

  > - Community-based accountability and good governance: Action taken at local level to ensure that rights holders enjoy their rights and that duty bearers are held accountable;
  > - National level: Focused more on influencing policy and practice at the national/international level, linked to learning generated from UMN's community-based programmes. (UMN, 2014c:35).

The 2015–2020 Strategic Plan strongly embraces a rights-based approach to development work. Although the strategy is built on what has been learnt over the last ten years, implementing it will involve some substantial shifts in thinking and practice. It will also require negotiating new ways of working with staff, local partners, supporting partners, and the Government of Nepal.

SETTING THE PLUMB-LINE (AMOS 7:8)

1. Organisational Change

Changing the way an organisation works is a long, slow process, requiring sustained commitment and effort (VeneKlasen et al., 2004:20). Developing new ways of working and ensuring consistency with flexibility is a huge challenge. Rights thinking needs to be "integrated into the fabric of the organisation" (Anderson, 2001:228). The way in which rights thinking is introduced has substantial impact. Harris-Curtis et al. list three ways of doing this (2005:19):

- A corporate decision;
- A bottom-up approach, led by local partners and field offices;
- A thematic approach, applied to particular work areas.

UMN's approach so far has been thematic: rights work and advocacy have been applied in particular contexts (disability work, women's groups, the PPP) or with particular communities (the Kumals). Although there has been input from field offices into the strategic planning process, the changes have not been *led* by them, and local partners have not been involved in the decision-making at all. The shift to a rights-based approach will be viewed as a corporate decision. Therefore, there is considerable risk that while senior staff are committed, new strategies and structures will not impact on day-to-day work unless fundamental changes occur in how we think about:

- *People.* The people involved in UMN projects must no longer be regarded as beneficiaries but as right-holders (Harris-Curtis et al. 2005:15, 30) or citizens (Walker, 2009:1046). The I/NGO's role is to "accompany" and support rather than provide. Meaningful participation thus becomes a key factor (VeneKlasen et al, 2004:10, 13ff). For UMN, this means working with partners to ensure that true participation at community level occurs.

- *Programmes.* The programmes UMN implements must move from a needs-based or service-delivery starting point to one that is truly driven by the communities we work with—or from "supply" to "demand" (Banks & Hulme, 2012:24). This is challenging, not just as a change in thinking, but in terms of structural and funding issues. VeneKlasen et al. warn against falling back into a narrow set of technical fixes (2004:42), instead of pursuing holistic transformation.

- *Power.* A rights-based approach shifts the power relationships between stakeholders. This is difficult, especially for educated, middle-class Nepalis in a hierarchical cultural context. It is also difficult for a large, established INGO, dealing with small, emergent NGOs and poor communities. For integrity and authenticity, the way the organisation operates should reflect its adherence to right and just relationships.

2. Staff Change

Staffing will be a key challenge. At the time of writing, most programme staff were selected because of their technical expertise in areas like health, education, livelihoods, etc. Few had solid training in community development, and even fewer in human rights or policy work. Staff need to be more multi-disciplinary, able to work in solidarity with people. They need to overcome the "culture of expertise" and become facilitators, rather than implementers (VeneKlasen et al., 2004:24–25; Walker, 2009:1050). Ife (2010:223ff) details the knowledge, values and skills he believes a community-based human rights practitioner needs. The list is daunting!

Rights-based approaches require "a new rigour and discipline in analysis, planning, implementing and monitoring and evaluating" (Harris-Curtis et al., 2005:22). Most development practitioners lack political awareness and policy knowledge (VeneKlasen et al., 2004:24), particularly when we consider national or international advocacy or campaigning.

These new skills cannot be acquired in a few internally-delivered training days. UMN must seek out longer-term training opportunities, for cluster and technical staff. It must invest in a carefully-planned staff development programme over several years. Training should deliver a sound understanding of community development practice, including rights-based approaches, and the capacity to work in advisory, capacity-building ways to support community empowerment.

3. Change in Partner Relationships

UMN prides itself on strong relationships with local partners. Staff work hard to support, encourage and develop organisational capacity. The 2015–2020 Strategic Plan requires many partners to work in different ways. These changes risk disempowering some partners and increase tensions, particularly if partners are not fully committed (Luttrel and Quiroz, 2007:3).

UMN will also need to provide or source for substantive training for partner leadership and staff; it is expensive and time-consuming, and weaker partners (including most of UMN's Christian partners) may struggle. A rights-based approach can also be risky for local partners, which are embedded in local communities, and can find that a more political stance causes difficulties with local elites (Harris-Curtis et al., 2005:37). Christian partners particularly have a lot to lose!

4. Donor and Constituency Change

UMN operates in a competitive global funding environment. Some donor organisations (sadly, particularly Christian organisations) are uncomfortable with rights-based approaches, preferring the "charity" model (VeneKlasen et al., 2004:21). Most donors measure success in terms of outputs from projects, not political change (Banks and Hulme, 2012:12). Even donors who say they are happy with rights-based approaches still require detailed logical-framework-based planning, often within terribly short timelines.[11]

---

11   Time and again, invitations to submit proposals are received with a response time of around two weeks. A round trip to many UMN working areas is about this long! Actually involving partner organisations in the process, let alone local communities, is often impossible due to these unrealistic deadlines.

In particular, supporting agencies that channel government funds from Western countries have difficulty with more open-ended approaches, and may face problems justifying support for activities that appear more political (Harris-Curtis et al., 2005:37). UMN receives government funds through INGOs from Australia, UK, Norway, Sweden, Germany and Finland. Many of these now have conservative governments, with (sometimes) a narrower view of development and greater scrutiny of international development funding.

Over the last 15 years, UMN's funding base has shifted from predominantly mission organisations to Christian development agencies. Feedback on the draft Strategic Plan 2015–2020 divided supporting partners roughly along these lines, with development agencies supportive, and with traditional missions (which mainly provide expatriates) less enthusiastic. However, even most of the former still fund on a project basis. A shift to "block funding", where donors support a strategy or a variety of work within a geographic area, is helpful, and some have moved in this direction.

Only 3 percent of UMN's support comes from individuals and churches, though these general constituencies are "back-donors" for supporting organisations. Rights-based approaches are more difficult to explain than basic human needs. Ordinary people are increasingly disengaged from poverty issues anyway (Danton and Kirk, 2011), and less likely to listen. Sadly, few supporting partners invest in the kind of constituency education pioneered by TEAR Australia (Bradbury, 2005). UMN strives to find creative and compelling ways to share the stories of change, enriching people's concept of development to include rights-based work, and helping secure support, both financial and prayer.

5. Government Relationships

Finally, one of the key challenges is maintaining good relationships with the Government of Nepal, at both local and national levels. The Government has expressed disapproval of words like "advocacy" in UMN's current strategy and Programme Agreement. However, a rights-based approach is acceptable to them, if couched in language that enables the Government to see that UMN is helping them fulfil their responsibilities. As an organisation dependent on the Government for its very existence, this is crucial for UMN.

THE DAYS ARE COMING (AMOS 8:11; 9:13)

The Kumals thought the day would never come when water would again flow through their irrigation channel onto their fields. Justice begins with seeing the *oppression* of the people, not just their poverty, and digging down into the roots of vulnerability that entangle communities like Pipaltar. When *the poor are deprived of justice*, bringing sound development practice and a rights-based approach together is crucial. Different ways of looking at the relationship can enrich our understanding and point us in new directions (Marks, 2003). Injustices that make and keep people like the Kumals poor and powerless are offensive to God, who calls us to *hate evil, do good and maintain justice*. This biblical imperative has driven UMN on its journey from *shepherd to prophet*, from service provider to capacity building to "pursuer of justice". The 2015–2020 Strategic Plan is challenging and ambitious, and requires substantive changes in thinking on the part of staff, partners, donors, and UMN itself. It propels UMN from "an implementer and driver of development" to relationships that create "allies and fellow partners in a collective struggle for change" (Chapman, 2005:7).

The days are coming...

These days,[12] Chintaman Kumal grows enormous cabbages in irrigated fields. Phulmaya Kumal is a trained community health worker at the Health Post, where Durga Nepali (18) has safely delivered her baby Nisa. The Child Club, led by Janak Kumal, is promoting sanitation and hygiene. Thakur Kumal and the Water Users' Committee direct the flow to Pipaltar and Majuwa in turn.

---

12   At the time of writing—2014.

So many other communities, scattered across the hills and plains of Nepal, are beaten down by injustice. The lack of land rights, water rights, the right to speak the local language, to live with dignity in spite of disability, to respect and safety in the home and to worthwhile, productive work, all contribute to poverty and hopelessness. As UMN takes up new and challenging ways of "addressing the root causes of poverty", and "pursuing peace and justice for all", we long to see "fullness of life for all, in a transformed Nepali society".

The days are coming...

REFERENCES

Anderson, Ian. 2001. "Northern NGO Advocacy: Perceptions, Reality and Challenge." Pp. 222–232 in *Debating Development: NGOs and the Future*, edited by Deborah Eade & Ernst Ligteringen. Oxford: Oxfam GB.

Banks, Nicole & Hulme, David. 2012. *The Role of NGOs and Civil Society in Development and Poverty Reduction*. BWPI Working Paper 171. Retrieved June 10, 2014. (http://hummedia.manchester.ac.uk/institutes/gdi/publications/workingpapers/bwpi/bwpi-wp-17112.pdf)

Booth, Beverley. 2009. *United Mission to Nepal Strategic Plan Process: 2001–2008*. Internal document.

Bradbury, Steve. 2005. "Educating for Compassion and Justice: TEAR Australia's Education Strategy." *Journal of Christian Education*. 48(3): 35–45.

Chapman, Jennifer. 2005. *Rights-Based Development: The Challenge of Change and Power*. Global Poverty Research Group, WPS-027.

Cornwall, Andrea. 2003. "Whose Voices? Whose Choices? Reflections on Gender and Participatory Development." *World Development*. 31(8): 1325–1342.

Darnton, Andrew & Kirk, Martin. 2011. Pp. 5–35 in *Finding Frames: New Ways to Engage the UK Public in Global Poverty*. Oxfam & UK Aid.

Harris-Curtis, Emma, Marleyn, Oscar & Bakewell, Oliver. 2005. *The Implications for Northern NGOs of Adopting Rights-Based Approaches*. INTRAC Occasional Papers Series (41).

IDS Policy Briefing. 2003. *The Rise of Rights: Rights-based Approaches to International Development*. 17. Retrieved February 20, 2020 (https://www.ids.ac.uk/publications/the-rise-of-rights-rights-based-approaches-to-international-development/)

Ife, Jim. 2010. *Human Rights from Below: Achieving Rights through Community Development*. Cambridge: Cambridge University Press.

Lorenzen, Thorwald. 2000. "Towards a Theology of Human Rights." *Review and Expositor*. 97: 49–66.

Luttrel, Cecilia & Quiroz, Sitna. 2007. *Linkages between Human Rights-based Approaches and Empowerment*. Retrieved October 23, 2014. (https://www.shareweb.ch/site/Poverty-Wellbeing/current povertyissues/Documents/Linkages%20between%20human%20rights-based%20approaches %20and%20empowerment%20-%20Cecilia%20Luttrell%20October%202007.pdf)

Maggay, Melba. 2005. *Religion, Human Rights and Development Co-operation: Some New Wineskins*. Conference on Religion: A Source for Human Rights and Development Cooperation, Soesterberg, The Netherlands, September 6–9 (unpublished).

Marks, Stephen P. 2005. "The Human Rights Framework for Development: Seven Approaches." Pp. 23–60 in *Reflections on the Right to Development*, edited by Arjun Sengupta, Archna Negi, Moushumi Basu. New Delhi: Sage Publications

Marshall, Christopher D. 2001. *Crowned with Glory and Honor: Human Rights in the Biblical Tradition*. Telford: Pandora Press.

Mott, Stephen Charles. 1982. *Biblical Ethics and Social Change*. New York, Oxford: OUP.

ODI Briefing Paper. 2001. *Economic Theory, Freedom and Human Rights: The Work of Amartya Sen*. Retrieved February 20, 2020. (https://www.odi.org/sites/odi.org.uk/files/odi-assets/publica tions-opinion-files/2321.pdf)

Padilla, Rene. 2009. "The Biblical Basis for Social Transformation". Pp. 187–204 in *Transforming the World?: The Gospel and Social Responsibility*, edited by Jamie A. Grant and Dewi Hughes. London: SPCK Publishing

Ramachandra, Vinoth. 2008. *Subverting Global Myths: Theology and the Public Issues Shaping our World.* Downers Grove, IL: InterVarsity Press.

Roy, Steven C. 2009. "Embracing Social Justice: Reflections from the Storyline of Scripture." *Trinity Journal.* 30(1): 3–48.

Sloane, Andrew. 2011. *Justifying Advocacy: A Biblical and Theological Rationale for Speaking the Truth to Power on Behalf of the Vulnerable.* The John Sanders Lecture.

Stackhouse, Max L. 2005. "Why Human Rights Need God: A Christian perspective." Pp. 25–40, *Does Human Rights Need God?*, edited by Elizabeth M. Bucar, & Barbara Marnett. Grand Rapids, MI: William B. Eerdmans.

Stassen, G.H. 2006. "The Kind of Justice Jesus Cares About." Pp. 157–176 in *Transforming the Powers: Peace, Justice, and the Domination System,* edited by R.C. Gingerich & T. Grimsrud. Minneapolis, MN: Fortress Press.

Thurley, Ben. 2011. "Christian Commitment to Building a New Nepal." Retrieved October 25, 2014. (https://www.umn.org.np/news/172)

UMN. 2002. *Strategic Plan 2003–2008.* Internal document.

---. 2006. *Mid-Term Review: 2003–2008 Strategic Plan.* Internal document.

---. 2010. *Strategic Plan 2010–2015.* Internal document.

---. 2014a. *UMN Advocacy Action Reflection, January 2014.* Internal document.

---. 2014b. *Cluster Report Case Stories, January–July 2014.* Internal document.

---. 2014c. *Strategic Plan 2015–2020.* Internal document.

---. 2014d. *Annual Report 2013–2014.* Internal document.

UN Declaration on the Right to Development. 1986. Retrieved October 14, 2014. (http://www.un.org/ga/search/view_doc.asp?symbol=a/res/41/128)

UNDP. 2014. *Nepal Human Development Report 2014.* Retrieved September 28, 2014. (http://www.np.undp.org/content/nepal/en/home/library/human_development/human-development-report-2014/)

VeneKlasen, Lisa, Miller, Valerie, Clark, Cindy & Reilly, Molly. 2004. *Rights-Based Approaches and Beyond: Challenges of Linking Rights and Participation.* IDS Working Paper 235, Brighton. (https://opendocs.ids.ac.uk/opendocs/handle/20.500.12413/4084)

Walker, David W. 2009. "Citizen-Driven Reform of Local-level Basic Services: Community-Based Performance Monitoring." *Development in Practice.* 19(8): 1035–1051.

Wieland, Alfonso. 2001. *In Love with His Justice.* Unpublished Paper given at Micah Network Triennial Consultation on Integral Mission, Oxford, UK. UK.

Williams, Rowan. 2012. *Theology and Human Rights in Moral Consciousness.* Archbishop of Canterbury lecture on Human Rights and Religious Faith at the World Council of Churches, Ecumenical Centre, Geneva — 28 February 2012. (https://www.oikoumene.org/en/press-centre/news/archbishop-of-canterbury-delivers-a-lecture-on-human-rights-and-faith)

Winterford, Keren. 2009. *Citizen Voice and Action Guidance Notes.* World Vision UK. (http://www.e-alliance.ch/typo3conf/ext/naw_securedl/secure0513.pdf?u=0&file=fileadmin/user_upload/docs/Advocacy_Capacity/2011/CitizenVoiceandActionGuidanceNotes.pdf)

World Food Program. 2014. Retrieved September 28, 2014. (https://www.wfp.org/countries/nepal)

Wright, Christopher. 2004. *Old Testament Ethics for the People of God.* Leicester: InterVarsity Press.

---. 2010. *The Mission of God's People: A Biblical Theology of the Church's Mission.* Grand Rapids, MI: Zondervan.

Appendix A: UMN's Mission and Vision Statements

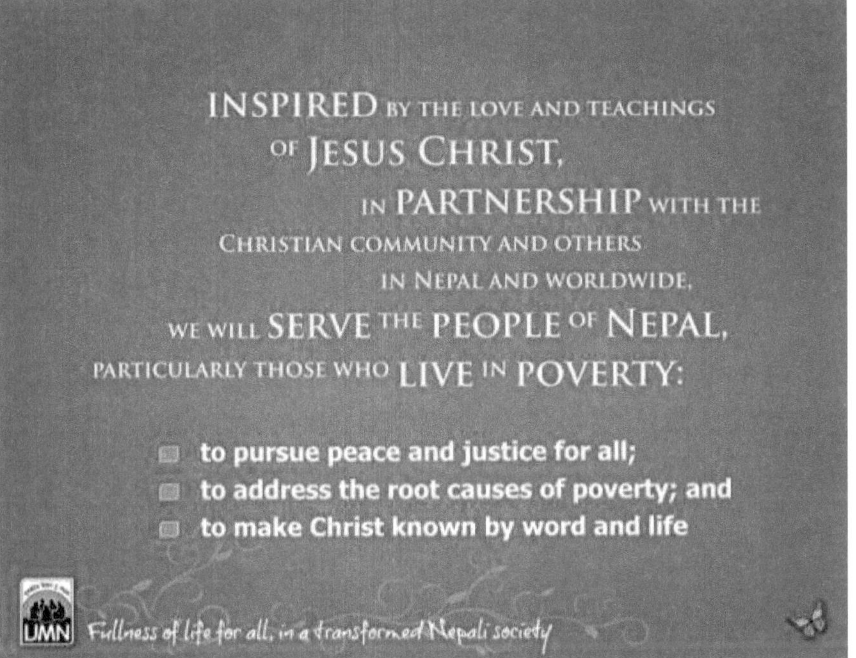

Appendix B: UMN's Fullness of Life Model

21st-century Modern-day Slavery: An Examination into Extreme Human Rights Abuse

Lee Soo Choo

Introduction

Slaves! The word conjures up vivid and horrible images of human suffering: men, women and children in chains, bodies bound in the bellies of dungeon ships, humans bought and sold as chattel in the marketplace. Recent movies have featured these historical depictions of slavery leading many of us to think of slavery as a thing of the past, safely and securely quarantined in history. Unfortunately, this is not the case. It has grotesquely morphed into new forms: forced labour, debt bondage, sex trafficking, child labour, forced marriages and involuntary domestic servitude. Even the dehumanising practice of branding remains. While slave owners in the past used a red hot iron to scorch their title of ownership on the body of a person, today, in the United States, "hundreds of women and children [...] have had their arms, backs, legs, faces, breasts and even eyelids and gums marked with pimp's names and gang tags or with barcodes, sexual slang words or dollar signs" (Kelly, 2014).

The Global Estimates of Modern Slavery, a collaborative research project by the International Labour Organization (ILO) and Walk Free Foundation in 2016, has revealed the true scale of modern slavery around the world. It asserts that there are an estimated 40.3 million people in modern slavery around the world, made up of:

- 10 million children;
- 24.9 million people in forced labour;
- 15.4 million people in forced marriage;
- 4.8 million people in forced sexual exploitation (ILO, 2017).

As a Malaysian, it is shocking for me to know that in 2018, my own nation was home to 212,000 people bonded in slavery, many of whom are domestic and sex workers (Global Slavery Index, 2018).

Definitions and Characteristics

Modern Slavery is an umbrella term referring to situations of exploitation that a person cannot refuse or leave because of threats, violence, coercion, deception, and/or abuse of power (ILO, n.d.).

Human trafficking is a form of modern-day slavery. It is an illegal act of the trading of people for exploitation and/or economic profit. The Malay word for human trafficking, *pemerdagangan orang*, literally translates to "trading people", and the Chinese character for it, 贩卖人口, comprises parts of words to do with transport and the sale of humans. Human trafficking takes the form of forced labour, bonded labour or debt bondage, sex trafficking, child labour, involuntary domestic servitude, or child soldiering. This crime can also be committed for the purpose of forced marriage or illegal adoption.

According to the United Nations' *Protocol to Prevent, Suppress and Punish Trafficking in Persons*,[1] trafficking in persons has three constituent elements:

---

1   This is often called the Palermo Protocol, it is one of the three protocols under The United Nations Convention against Transnational Organized Crime, adopted by General Assembly resolution 55/25 of 15 November 2000, the main international instrument in the fight against transnational organised crime.

The Act (what is done): recruitment, transportation, transfer, harbouring or receipt of persons;

The Means (how it is done): threat or use of force, coercion, abduction, fraud, deception, abuse of power or vulnerability, or giving payments or benefits to a person in control of the victim;

The Purpose (why it is done): for the purpose of exploitation, which includes exploiting the prostitution of others, sexual exploitation, forced labour, slavery or similar practices and the removal of organs (UNODC, 2020).

Human trafficking is the second most profitable illegal industry—second only to the drug trade. Forced labour in the private economy generates US$150 billion in illegal profits per year, about three times more than previously estimated in ILO findings. The 2014 ILO report, *Profits and Poverty: The Economics of Forced Labour*, reveals that two-thirds of the estimated total, US$99 billion, came from commercial sexual exploitation, while another US$51 billion resulted from forced economic exploitation, including domestic work, agriculture and other economic activities (ILO, 2014). We can see that trafficking in persons is driven by high rewards with low risks, as lasting legal consequences for human traffickers are still extremely minimal. According to Richard Holbrooke, former US Ambassador to the UN, "Slavery is a slippery and confounding evil and persists, despite 12 international conventions banning the slave trade, and over 300 international treaties banning slavery" (Skinner, 2008:9–10).

Multiple forms of injustice and human rights violations are the generators of today's slavery, including unregulated exploitation of workers, gender inequality, poverty, domestic violence, etc. Much of it, and sex trafficking in particular, is linked to organised crime. According to David Batstone, "It is clear that the Russian mafia has its stamp on practically every facet of sex trafficking trade in Eastern Europe. Its home base is massive, linking thousands of organisations including otherwise illegitimate businesses. And their influence goes beyond, to Israel, western Europe, US, Canada and Southeast Asia" (2007:177). The extent of their reach carries with it a reputation of ruthless use of violence.

Trafficking is lucrative because "once a drug is sold, it's gone, but a girl can be sold and used over and over before she collapses, has gone mad, commits suicide or dies of disease", a British Columbian man convicted of trafficking once said.[2] This confession reveals the ruthless and truly evil logic that drives human trafficking. People made in God's own image are rendered disposable, like used batteries. Once the slave exhausts his or her usefulness, another can be procured at no great expense (Batstone, 2007:11). Consider, for example, the trafficked fishermen in the South China Sea. They were confined in a vessel at sea for three years, tossed overboard if they fell ill, and harshly beaten up. They also "[became] the 'human stress-buster' [...] and were forced to line up in front of the captains for their traditional game of Russian roulette—shoot the fishermen" (Tenaganita, 2009:70).

In the modern-day slave trade, "the 'glut of slaves' and the capacity to move them great distances in a relatively short period of time drastically alters the economics of slave ownership" (Batstone, 2007:11). These days, a tragic side-effect of the lower cost of international flights has been the increased vulnerability of children in poor communities in Asia to the predatory behaviour of foreign paedophiles.

With the rise of the internet, social media has been increasingly used by predators to contact, recruit, and sell children for sex, according to a study by The University of Toledo Human Trafficking and Social Justice Institute (University of Toledo, 2018). Traffickers use love and affection as control mechanisms. Research and direct evidence also show that technology is being misused by human traffickers during all the stages of the crime, including recruitment, control, and exploitation of victims (ICAT, 2019). The passing of two United States house bills—FOSTA, the Fight Online Sex Trafficking Act, and the Senate bill, SESTA, the Stop Enabling Sex Traffickers Act in 2018—have been hailed by advocates as a victory for sex-trafficked victims (Kahveci, 2018).

---

2   The information can be found in this set of slides: http://bit.ly/11owOT8. Accessed 21 Nov 2014.

In 2016, Al Jazeera's 101 East programme exposed the sinister world of baby selling in Malaysia, where infants are sold online to the highest bidder (2016). Some babies are bought by couples desperate to start a family. Others are sold to traffickers and forced to become sex slaves or beggars. This brings us to another allegation where sex workers' babies are sold for up to RM40,000 while rejected babies are returned to syndicates to be brought up as future sex workers (Tenaganita, 2016a).

We may think that modern slavery does not really affect us, but sadly it is not so. Slave labour contributes to the production of at least 122 goods from 58 countries worldwide (*The Straits Times*, 2014). Since slavery feeds directly into the global economy, it makes sense that we should be concerned by the ways in which slavery flows into our homes through the products we buy and the investments we make. Items like coffee, sugar, rice, and cotton are tainted, while some seafood, especially shrimp, is harvested by children under unbelievably abusive conditions. Christmas tree ornaments sold at Walmart and other retail shops in the United States were made in a Chinese sweatshop that employed workers as young as 12 and others who work more than 100 hours a week (Fight Slavery Now, n.d.). The Modern Slavery Act of 2015 has since required British companies over a certain size to report on slavery in their supply chains, and Australia has just made it law in 2018 (Home Affairs, 2018).

CONTRIBUTING FACTORS

One of the main contributing factors to the rise of modern day slavery is the economic and social disparities caused by rapid social and economic change, mass displacement, conflict, and increased urbanisation, where people have no "safety net" and no job security. A recent example is the rural and poor province of Nghe An of Vietnam, a place targeted by people smugglers with well-connected underground networks across the world. They prey on poor desperate families who take huge loans to send their young away to find a better life elsewhere. Unfortunately these families' dreams were shattered, when they found out that their sons and daughters were among the 39 people found dead in a refrigerator trailer in London in a 2019 trafficking tragedy (Khidhir, 2019).

Another grievous factor is government corruption around the world, allowing slavery to go unpunished, even though it is illegal everywhere.[3] Malaysia's failure to initiate prosecution and conviction of complicit government officials is one of the major reasons it still remains in the Tier 2 Watch List (second worst grade) (US Embassy, 2019). In May 2015, news shook the world, when police discovered 139 graves, 106 bodies, believed to be Rohingyas, and 29 illegal immigrant detention camps deep in the jungles of the Malaysia-Thai border, in Wang Kelian. In 2017, an exhaustive, two-year investigation by the *New Straits Times* (NST) into these mass killings has revealed startling new evidence that suggests a massive, coordinated cover-up, including the destruction of evidence (2017). This report exposed the blatant complicity of the authorities in such horrific criminal activities.

Forms and Impact of Human Trafficking

Forced labour is a catch-all term used by ILO to denote slave-like working conditions. This form of exploitation is one of the most common motivations for human trafficking. The ILO Forced Labour Convention, 1930 (No. 29) defined forced or compulsory labour as "all work or service which is exacted from any person under the threat of a penalty and for which the person has not offered himself or herself involuntarily" (ILO, n.d.).

In 2014, the Verite research revealed concrete evidence of widespread forced labour among foreign migrant workers in the Malaysian electronics industry, defining it as systemic exploitation. This confirmed previous reports that established that one in three foreign workers in Malaysia was in a condition of forced labour.[4] (The laptop I am using now may well be a product of forced labour!) The 2016 Global Slavery Index asserted

---

3   https://www.freetheslaves.net/Document.Doc?id=21. Accessed 21 Nov 2014.

4   The full report of the research can be found at http://www.verite.org/sites/default/files/images/VeriteForcedLaborMalaysianElectronics_2014_0.pdf. Accessed 20 Nov 2014.

that over 128,000 workers in Malaysia were employed in slave-like conditions and treated like livestock, of which the majority (as with other richer Asian countries) were young girls and women migrants working as domestic helpers. They have been subjected to inhumane treatment, including starvation and physical and sexual abuse. On top of this, there is evidence of forced labour, extortionate recruitment fees, confinement to the place of employment, excessive unpaid overtime, the withholding of wages, and the confiscation of passports to prevent escape (Tenaganita, 2016b). Workers are often powerless, and at the mercy of their employers and recruiting agents. Physical assault can result in debilitating injuries and food deprivation can lead to sickness and incapacity.

The number of coffins with dead migrant workers that leave Malaysia is simply appalling. Every day in 2018, a Nepali migrant worker died in Malaysia. The figure was just as bad in 2017, with 364 deaths (Balasegaram, 2019). A total of 5,982 Nepali migrant workers have died in 29 destination countries during the fiscal years 2008 to 2017. Of these, the highest number of deaths (36%) occurred in Malaysia. A report from a recent consultation on emerging health issues of Nepali migrant workers in Malaysia indicated that there is some evidence of an association between sudden cardiac death and the risk factors experienced by the migrant workers, such as long working hours, exposure to extreme temperature and strenuous physical activity (Aryal et al., 2019).

Death would be the ultimate impact, if not a welcomed relief to the horrendous suffering of trafficked refugees! "Sold like fish: Crimes against Humanity, Mass Graves, and Human Trafficking from Myanmar and Bangladesh to Malaysia" is a joint report by the Human Rights Commission of Malaysia (Suhakam) and Fortify Rights (Reliefweb, 2019). As the title suggests, the report documents human rights violations perpetrated against Rohingya Muslims trafficked from Myanmar and Bangladesh to Thailand and Malaysia from 2012 to 2015, the discovery of mass graves in Wang Kelian, and analyses the violence against the victims within the framework of relevant international law. A 17-year-old survivor of those trafficking camps reported that "after two months, the people who couldn't give money—the people who were still there started dying". They were tortured with pipes, bats, clubs, belts, tasers, threats and intimidation. Denial of food, water and space resulted in deaths, illness, injury and paralysis. What a tragic denial of our common humanity, and what terrible shame, Malaysia, Myanmar and Thailand! Are they crying for justice like in the days of Job when "the groans of the dying rise from the city, and the souls of the wounded cry out for help"? (Job 24:12, NIV).

Compared to forced labour and debt bondage victims, there are additional elements of abuse that confront sex-trafficked victims. Firstly, she suffers a violation, an intrusion into her body, which damages her dignity and psychological well-being. Secondly, she suffers from social contempt and shame, as a result of being a sexually abused victim. In fact, their internalisation of this "bad woman" image is "one of the most effective chains tying women into sex work. These women and girls carry the heaviest burden of sexual double standards" (Brown, 2000:246). In Bangladesh, the prostitutes were so ostracised that they were neither allowed to wear shoes in public nor allowed to bury or cremate their dead—the bodies are just thrown into the river (ibid).

The Khmer proverb "Men are gold, women are cloth" encapsulates this mentality that pervades most Asian societies. A young Cambodian woman explained the proverb in a 1993 study, "The men look like gold. When it drops in mud we can clean it, but the women look like white clothes; when it drops in mud, we cannot clean it and be white again"[5] (Brown, 2000:246).

In my five years of involvement with survivors at the Tenaganita Shelter, I have interacted with girls who were scraped with sharp objects, scalded with hot water, bitten by guard dogs, sexually violated, refused contact with family, and financially and socially abused. There were those who suffered abuse amounting to vaginal, oral and anal rape, unwanted pregnancies, forced/botched abortions—leading to health consequences

---

5   The 1993 study is from Phan and Patterson, *Men are Gold, Women are Cloth* (CARE International in Cambodia, 1994) 19; quoted in Louise Brown's, *Sex Slaves: the Trafficking of Women in Asia* (London, UK: Virago Press, 2000).

like sexually transmitted diseases, pelvic infections, damage to organs and HIV/AIDS (Tenaganita, n.d.). Practically every one of them was mentally traumatised, struggling with anger, shame, guilt and disempowerment. We had an immigrant bride from Vietnam, bought and abused by a retired Malaysian man twice her age. There was girl from India who was cheated and forced into serving sex to migrant workers. She faced the dilemma of returning home to her village in India, fearing the stigma and consequences of punishment from her husband and conservative family, and yet wanting to warn the girls in her village, so they would not fall into the same trap. Having witnessed such debasement and suffering I can readily understand why this despicable human trade is called a scourge and a crime against humanity. The Second Vatican Council cited the Gaudium et Spes, which decries acts of slavery as "infamies which poison human society, debase their perpetrators and constitute a supreme dishonour to the Creator" (Kralis, 2006).

We can safely say that the trafficking of women and children constitutes the worst form of violations of human rights. As noted in a report by the Human Rights Commission of Malaysia, "the perpetrators violate the universal rights of all persons to life, liberty and freedom. It is an obstacle to the achievement of the objectives of equality and development. It impairs or nullifies the enjoyment by women and children of their basic human rights and fundamental freedoms" (Suhakam, 2004:4).

An important consideration is that the demand side of this billion-dollar industry is a direct result of the growing tourism industry, migration patterns and local demand for the "services" provided in Malaysia. The growing demand for sex with children and the existence of migrant children vulnerable to human traffickers has only complicated the fight against the scourge (2019), says Tenaganita. One reason for this demand is the belief that children are free from sexually transmitted diseases, especially HIV and AIDS, and being so young, presumably able to be used for years to come, they are therefore considered long-term investments!

The tremendous harm to children cannot be over exaggerated, as trafficking of children "affronts the basic need of a child to grow up in a safe and protective environment and free from exploitation and abuse. Apart from gross violations of human rights, it threatens the world by allowing a safehaven for trafficking syndicates, funding illicit activities and facilitating the spread of sexually transmitted diseases including HIV/AIDS".[6]

BIBLICAL REFLECTIONS

Slavery and human trafficking are not new. The story of Joseph in the Bible, tells how he was sold by his brothers (Gen. 37:28). The prophet Amos describes poor people being sold, trampled on, denied justice and oppressed by their own people (Amos 2:6–7). The defeated nation of Israel was scattered and its people were traded (Joel 3:3). Set free from slavery in Egypt, the Israelites were called to live differently as God's covenanted people, never to forget what it was like to be enslaved (Lev. 19:33–34).

On Slavery

In his analysis of Old Testament laws governing the treatment of slaves in Israel, Christopher Wright concludes that our translation of the Hebrew *'ebed*, which meant bonded labourer, as slave is unhelpful, because the *'ebed* enjoyed more explicit legal and economic security than the technically free, but landless, hired labourers and craftsmen (2004:333).

Slaves were included in the religious life of the community (Exod. 12:44), the Sabbath rest (Exod. 20:10), and were provided the protection of civil law (Exod. 20:21–27). These factors, along with other related Old Testament laws, provide evidence of a "deep concern for the personal humanity and physical integrity of the slave, which had been assaulted" (Wright, C: 2004:334). They were even given choices to stay or leave (Deut. 15:13–17).

Another unique law is the law of asylum in Deuteronomy 23:15–16, which, according to Wright, is "one of the most countercultural pieces of Old Testament legislation to be found, where the law not only allowed

6   Paper presented by Her Excellency Maria T. Huhtala, former Ambassador of the US to Malaysia, at the Forum on Trafficking of Women and Children, 13–14 April 2004.

runaway slaves freedom; it went beyond that and commanded their protection" (Wright, 2004:336), something unheard of in the neighbouring societies of that time.

Behind all these laws was the fundamental conviction and truth affirmed in Job 31:15 regarding both master and slave, "Did not he who made me (Job the master) in the womb make them (the slaves in his household)? Did not the same one form us both within our mothers?" (NIV) Slave and master—both God-made, and both made in God's own image. This same conviction informed Paul's assertion that slave and free are one in Christ (Gal. 3:28).

On Work Ethics

There is a deep and detailed concern in the Old Testament with work and employment, in respect to conditions and terms of service, adequate rest, and fair play (Wright, 2004:160). This cuts across the whole spectrum: employers, slaves, hired workmen, and even animals (Exod. 23:4–5; Deut. 25:4)!

Bonded workers who had voluntarily entered the service of a creditor because of inability to support themselves were not to be made to work in oppressively harsh conditions. (Lev. 25:39–40, 43) The wages of hired workers were to be paid fully and promptly (Lev. 19:13; Deut. 24:14–15). The prophets warned against oppression and exploitation of workers (Isa 58:3; Jer. 22:13). Sabbath rest was made mandatory for employers, employees and even animals (Exod. 20:11). All Sabbath institutions (jubilee release, release of pledges) "were concerned with the interest of workers, especially those whose only asset was their labour" (Wright, 2004:159).

It is important to note that the Bible describes vulnerable people as oppressed and downtrodden, rather than label them as "unfortunates". The latter implies that nobody is responsible for their condition, that nobody is guilty, while the former indicates the need for justice, for laws to protect their rights (Wolterstorff, 2013:77).

We see above how these sets of laws or "rules" on how to treat employees were not left to the powerful and influential to determine according to their whims and fancies. No, they were set down in the revealed Word of God, and those who ignored them placed themselves under God's condemnation.

On Human Rights

The clear testimony of Scripture is that all humans are made in the image of God, and it is this which accords each and every person inherent value and dignity. From a Christian perspective, the universality of human rights, therefore, is not based on "the common attributes of human nature or the common interests of human communities, but on the existence and character of one God who imparts his image equally to every human being" (Marshall, 2002:61). As a consequence, when we stand before another person, however destitute, disabled, diseased or degraded, we stand before something that is the vehicle of the divine (Ramachandra, 2008:104–105). Their oppression or neglect is "a sin against the Creator; their abuse is sacrilege, the desecration of something most holy, the violation of God in person" (Marshall, 2002:62). Here we can see why modern slavery is an offence to God: it dehumanises the victims, denies them their God-given value and worth, and robs them of dignity and autonomy.

The Quartet of Vulnerable and the Preferential Option for the Poor

The Bible identifies particular groups of vulnerable people, orphans, widows, aliens, the economically poor (Jer. 22:2–5), and those who cannot speak for themselves (Prov. 31:8). These people receive God's special attention "because they are the ones who are on the "wronged" side of a situation of chronic injustice—a situation that God abhors and wishes to have redressed" (Wright, 2004:268).

As Wolterstorff pointed out, all of us, rich or poor, may suffer episodes of injustice. But for vulnerable people, their daily condition is systemically unjust (or highly vulnerable to being systemically unjust), hence God's preferential option for the poor (Wolterstorff, 2013:77).

God's preferential option for the poor is also demonstrated in the person and work of Jesus Christ, who announced himself as the one anointed by the Spirit "to bring good news to the poor" (Luke 4:18–19 NLT). In Christ, God identified not only with the poor but also with those denied justice. His own trial was riddled with illegalities—a grave miscarriage of justice (Keller, 2013:186). In this way Jesus "identifies with millions of nameless people who have been wrongfully imprisoned, robbed of their possessions, tortured and slaughtered" (ibid.).

The ultimate instance of God's identification with the oppressed and vulnerable is at the Cross, where "he not only became one of the actually poor and marginalised, he stood in the place of all those of us in spiritual poverty and bankruptcy (Matt. 5:3) and paid our debt" (Keller, 2010:188).

Injustice as Abuse of Power

According to Rene Padilla, God's justice "applies to every form of abuse of power, unjust economic distribution, or violation of human rights present in society [...] It embraces every human relationship and seeks to abolish every manifestation of injustice. It is corrective, rectifying and restorative justice" (McLaren et al., 2009:25).

Injustice occurs when power is misused to take from others what God has given them, namely their life, dignity, liberty or the fruits of their love and labour (Haugen, 1999:73). Hence modern slavery is clearly a gross injustice and an abuse of power. Conversely, justice is the right use of power in our relationships with others. Justice is "what power is for in God's economy: the bringing of blessing for whom it is to be exercised through the establishing of justice, through the use of power to establish, restore and maintain right relationships in the community [...] a pattern by which all users of earthly power are held accountable by God" (Sloane, 2011:6).

It is heartening to see the United Nations using power rightly as it pursues justice through its comprehensive, human-rights-based strategies to combat human trafficking, and moves beyond the protection of victims, to the prosecution and prevention of this crime. Since 2009, the UN Special Rapporteur Report on trafficking in persons, especially women and children (n.d.), has expanded the vision from three P's to five P's, of Prevention, Prosecution, Punishment, Protection and Promotion (of international cooperation). And it has adopted a victim-centred approach through the three R's—Redress, Rehabilitation/Recovery and Re-integration. Malaysia has since adopted this approach, though it will take time, courage and political will for this to take shape.

Warning to Rulers

God has clearly commanded political leaders (of nations and tribes), to **speak up** for the voiceless, to **defend** the rights of all who are afflicted and destitute, to **rescue** the weak, the poor and needy, to **free** them from the hand of the wicked, not to **pervert justice** (Ps. 82:2–4; Prov. 31:8–9; Deut. 16:18–20). The Psalmist pleaded with God to give the king God's heart for justice, "to **bring deliverance** to the children of the needy, to **crush** the oppressor!" (Ps. 72:1–4). Failure to protect the weak, to uphold justice will certainly incur God's wrath, as seen in Jeremiah 22:2–5, "But if you do not obey these commands, declares the Lord, I swear by myself that this palace will become a ruin". This poses a severe warning to institutions or governments who neglect their duty to protect the vulnerable, or who by turning a blind eye effectively sanction systemic slavery.

We gather from the above reflections that the Biblical mandate to do justice, to love mercy, is very clear. The continuing horrors of modern slavery that mar the image of God's creation demands an urgent response from the people of God.

RESPONSE

The Exposed Campaign in 2013 (WEA, n.d.), a global Christian call to action against corruption that robs the poorest of our world, had as its slogan: Corruption Has a Name. Poverty Has a Face. You Have a Voice.

A face is personal. A face belongs to a human person with dignity and intrinsic value. It is not an abstraction attached to a mere statistic. A face has a name, a personality, a family, a story.

Ah Bee was barely 16 years old when she was brought to us at the Tenaganita Shelter[7] around 2008. She had been picked up from the streets, distraught and without documents. The big maroon scar on her left arm will always remind her of the horrors of a dog unleashed on her when she tried to escape. She remembered she was Burmese, sold when she was just a few years old to Thai men, and later brought down to the East Coast of Malaysia, where she was used and abused till her heart and mind could not withstand the brutality anymore. The trauma was too deep and devastating for her to recover fully. For me, Ah Bee represents the haunting face of global trafficking.

Poverty has a face, and we have a voice—a voice to speak for the downtrodden, to speak and act prophetically to "set the prisoners free", and to challenge the social, economic and political factors that create the conditions necessary for the evil trade in human lives.

We Have a Voice

In 2010 my pastor asked me to write a reflection on the Lord's Prayer for our local Lutheran Newsletter. It triggered a significant and deeply personal moment of new understanding: that the Lord's prayer is not just a prayer about my personal needs, but a communal prayer, one that concerns itself with the food and daily bread of all people everywhere. It enfolds all who suffer oppression within its yearnings, and it became my lament. God used his prayer to channel my anger at oppression and injustice into prayers and action. That was my awakening.

Christians need to be awakened—from ignorance and apathy, from church-club mentalities or bad theologies—to the issues of poverty, justice and compassion around us. As Timothy Keller pointed out, there is a heart for the poor that is dormant in a Christian's soul that needs to be

---

7   Tenaganita is a human rights NGO in Malaysia. They started a shelter for trafficked women and children in 2006, of which I was the manager from 2006–2011.

awakened, because of grace and not guilt (2010:107). More people need to discover that "a passion for Jesus ought to result in a passion for justice" (Bradbury, S. 2005:35).

Church leaders need to be infected by the biblical passion and vision for justice. Imagine the impact on churches of impassioned teaching about the biblical foundations of justice, or Jesus' mission to set the oppressed free! It would build the capacity of their members to stand up for those who need protection. Churches could incorporate awareness education on modern slavery issues into their training and discipleship programmes and seminaries—excellent resources are freely available on-line.

Speaking up would also mean church leaders preaching sermons that address serious ethical issues relevant to our contexts: our work ethics, how we treat our domestic workers (do we, for example, allow them a proper rest day?), how we deal with supply chains in our businesses that involve slave labour. Keller tells the story of a textile worker in Hong Kong, who, despite recognising his own sinfulness, rejected the message of the church because the message he heard was only about private sins and left out the social sins, e.g. the sins of his employer, the usage of child labour, false labels, forced overtime and withholding valid leave (2010:56). Keller highlighted that many of the management class were sitting in the same congregation, and the pastor was not willing to broach the issue of ethical behaviour in the workplace for fear of losing their tithes and offerings!

Jim Ife states that "one of the most effective forms of human rights education is through modelling human rights [...] it is how people are treated that makes a lasting impression: whether it is kindness or cruelty" (2010:204). This would mean that church folks start to model human rights by treating their own domestic workers with respect, dignity and fairness.

Very few Christian entities in Malaysia are involved in justice and anti-trafficking issues. The Global Shepherds (formerly Good Shepherd Services) does excellent work in running shelters, outreach programmes, counselling & empowerment programmes for survivors of abuse. Change Your World (CYW) is a unique Christian organisation committed to empowering the next generation of youths to tackle real-world social issues like human trafficking. In 2015 Change Your World, in partnership with Tenaganita and members of the Selangor State government, launched the Be My Protector campaign, primarily through social media. It reached out to more than 500,000 people to highlight the importance of fighting human trafficking (Tenaganita, 2018). In 2018, the same campaign created an app (with eight languages), the first in Southeast Asia (Tham, 2018), offering everyone in Malaysia the opportunity to submit reports of abuses safely, anonymously and quickly, to case workers who were proven reliable and experienced.

In 2016, when reports of Bangladeshi students in Malaysia being cheated became one too many, a group of young journalists decided to take action. They spent a year of undercover investigation, and discovered that the students were victims of a recruitment system embedded in a wicked million-dollar trade that was leaving a trail of devastated lives (Yee et al., n.d.). In a callous pursuit of profit, the recruiters lied to, exploited, extorted these vulnerable students who were eventually left with no education. The journalists' award-winning documentary series "Desperate in Dhaka" (True Story Award, n.d.), their reports and their campaign for justice have not only created awareness and resulted in prosecutions—they have also saved many others from further exploitation.

These two stories are contemporary examples of how anyone can be involved to create awareness. The Lausanne Covenant recommends young people to take up careers that will help protect and care for the abused. Lawyers, artists, musicians, writers, producers, missionaries, relief and development workers, social workers, and counsellors, all can use their voice and skills to protect and advocate for trafficked victims (George, 2014). SK!N: A new work in contemporary performance based around true stories about Human Trafficking[8] is a good example of how artists can be passionately involved to bring to light the silenced voices of victims. After premiering in Malaysia in 2016, these local and international artists

---

8   http://www.tenaganita.net/events/skn/

are taking these stories of resilience and hope to other parts of the world, to Asia Pacific, Europe and United States.

The Church is God's agent for transformation and is mandated to bring shalom and justice into the brokenness and oppression in the world. The global Church has a strong voice that can lobby local and federal governments for allocation of resources to combat trafficking, raise awareness and create demands for justice, and lobby international and local businesses to monitor and clean up their supply chains (George, 2014). The Lutheran World Federation, the World Council of Churches, the World Evangelical Alliance and regional bodies like Christian Conference Asia (CCA) and others have all spoken up against the crimes and are advocating for change. However, this cry for justice and reparation needs to filter down to local church bodies. I was very encouraged by our first-ever Inter-Faith Joint Declaration in Malaysia, in 2017, where 11 leaders from different religions came together to pledge to fight trafficking by working for the freedom of victims, to restore their dignity and give them a reason to hope once more (CCMalaysia, 2017). This initiative, spearheaded by the Catholic Archdiocese of Kuala Lumpur in collaboration with the Conference of Religious Major Superiors Malaysia-Singapore-Brunei, to garner inter-faith collaboration (including Evangelical Christian and Muslim groups), is quite exceptional. As unity is strength, I hope that this collaboration can become a stronger voice to lobby for better measures to fight this evil crime.

In 2014, Malaysia was downgraded to the lowest tier,[9] on par with countries like Zimbabwe and North Korea, because the country failed to comply with the most basic international requirements to prevent trafficking and protect victims within its borders. This is the third time in seven years, since 2007 and 2009. Malaysia stands accused of putting the needs of business, employers and agents before the needs of trafficked victims, which comprise the vast majority of Malaysia's estimated two million illegal migrant labourers, working in the agriculture, construction,

---

9   The Malaysian Anti-trafficking in Persons Report 2014 can be accessed at http://www. state.gov/documents/organization/226847.pdf.

sex, textile or domestic labour industries.[10] It has "created a system where unscrupulous labour brokers, corrupt police and abusive employers can have a field day", says Phil Robertson, Asia's deputy director of Human Rights Watch.

In 2019, we are still on the Tier 2 watch list, just half a notch better. Corruption related to processes for foreign labour remains pervasive and the government has stopped funding NGOs to provide shelter for victims. The two National Action Plans, the opening up of special courts to speed up prosecution and the ratifying of the ASEAN Convention Against Trafficking in persons, especially Women and Children, are signs of a greater effort and determination of the Malaysian government to reach Tier 1 in 2020. The church, in partnership with civil societies and NGOs, can play a part in holding governments responsible, to lobby for stiffer laws and penalties for perpetrators, proper reintegration of survivors and their involvement in the drafting of policies or issues of anti-human trafficking.

Doing Responsible Business

Forced labour is often hidden, sometimes found many steps down the supply chain, buffered by outsourcing companies or agents. Hence, businesses can remain ignorant of the full extent of slavery in their supply chains. Action is needed to address this—such as the British Government's Modern Slavery Act of 2015, which requires British companies over a certain size to report on slavery in their supply chains.

This is a good beginning, but according to Monique Villa, CEO of Thomson Reuters Foundation, "the real impact comes from cross-sector collaboration and shared expertise, with businesses, government and civil society working together" (Villa, 2018). In other words, we can be more effective by sharing data to develop best practices and address the gaps and loopholes that keep forced labour alive. An excellent example of such collaboration is the Better Cotton Initiative, a global cotton

---

10   http://www.theguardian.com/global-development/2014/jun/20/malaysia-us-human-traffickingpersons-report. Accessed 23 Nov 2014.

sustainability programme, which unites everyone from farmers to fashion brands in raising the standards of global cotton production.[11] The goal is to improve working conditions, have a lower environmental impact and, overall, strengthen the sector's competitiveness. Another is the Responsible Business Alliance,[12] a coalition of businesses working in the electronics industry committed to supporting the rights of workers and communities linked to their supply chains. Last but not least, the Global Business Coalition Against Human Trafficking (GBCAT) is a collaborative initiative that aims to harness the power of business across sectors to prevent and reduce the incidence of modern slavery and to support survivors in their reintegration into the workforce, with member companies like Amazon, Google, Microsoft and Coca-Cola.[13]

Since slave labour is often in the supply chain for popular goods, consumers, too, have a role to play in ethical purchasing. As Christians we can make informed choices that align with Kingdom values, to purchase slave-free or fair-trade products. We can also report cases when supply chains were tainted with usage of slave labour, as in the example of a Good Samaritan sister, who reported that religious items like crosses, Bible-covers and t-shirts were made by child slaves, working up to 19-hour days seven days a week, for a couple of dollars a day (Catholic Leader, 2009). According to the article, "The seriousness of the issue has led the National Council of Churches in Australia to pledge its support for a Christian Goods Standard to end worker exploitation" (ibid.). It has also prompted the development of The Just Holy Hardware campaign, which includes a website to promote fair-trade. Here we see how awareness and reporting can lead to concrete action against forced labour.

Restoring Lives

Because of the multiple adverse impacts on survivors of modern slavery, their recovery is usually a long process of rehabilitation, legal redress and

---

11   https://bettercotton.org/
12   http://www.responsiblebusiness.org/
13   https://www.greenbiz.com/article/three-ways-business-combating-modern-slavery

safe repatriation. But I have had the privilege of seeing some of them smile again, witnessing their joy in recovery and reunification with families. I have seen how church networks in the ASEAN Region have assisted in reporting abuse and facilitating the safe re-integration of survivors. God's people can certainly play a role in the healing processes that rebuild dignity and self-esteem. They can help develop new vocational opportunities through the volunteering of time and expertise, and by marketing and purchasing survivor-made products. During my time at the Tenaganita Shelter, we had a variety of volunteers, one of whom was a dancer who used movement to help survivors express themselves. These girls not only had fun but also the thrill and excitement of performing at the NGO's One Day Off Campaign for Domestic Workers and other awareness-raising events.

Addressing the Powers That Be

We know that governments have a responsibility to serve the general welfare of the people they govern. Just as the rulers and kings of biblical times were mandated by God to rule justly, so are today's governments and institutions. According to Walter Wink, these powers (governments, corporations, etc.) are not simply people and institutions, but also have a spiritual core, and therefore, "if we want to change those systems, we will have to address not only their outer forms, but their inner spirit as well" (1998:4).

Taking on the "powers that be", the god of Mammon, or the Market-god, and speaking truth to power, are part of our job description as people of faith. Many secular organisations are doing a great job handling the "outer forms" of decay, and we need to be alongside them in that. But we who have been awakened in a spiritual sense need to "[keep] praying, for even one more day is too long to wait for justice" (Wink, 1998:195). Pleading with God for the transformation of the institutions and structures that promote slavery is an integral and vital dimension of our participation in that process.

Keeping Hope Alive

The massive scale of modern slavery and the horrendous impact on its victims can be numbing and depressing, sometimes creating a sense of helplessness and hopelessness.

In his experience fighting against human trafficking, Gary Haugen, the director of International Justice Mission (IJM) realised that "The battle against oppression stands or falls in the battlefield of hope" (Haugen, 1999:67). We need "a hope that has power to prevail against the worst that hell can bring to earth [...] as nothing challenges one's faith and hope in God like the rank evil of naked injustice [...] and nothing short of the authority, divine Word of God will withstand its withering scorn" (Haugen, 1999:68–69). We have to keep this hope alive and not let despair overcome us, as this can have rippling effects on those working alongside us. The Church must preach a gospel of hope, a hope that contends with the ugly darkness of our world, a "gospel that changes the self-understanding of the poor, that their life is not defined by the injustice or poverty, but by hope in Christ" (Haugen, 1999:104). The work of justice requires sustained energy, patience, hope and endurance for the long haul.

Hope is what made Elisabeth, a 16-year-old trafficked victim, write Psalm 27:1–3 on the wall of the cell where she was serially raped day after day, "The Lord is the stronghold of my life [...] though an army besiege me, my heart will not fear, though war break out against me, even then will I be confident" (Crouch, n.d.).

I derive hope from the example of Zach Hunter who, at the age of 12, started a fundraising campaign to collect loose change to fund rescues for modern-day slaves. His initiative inspired a student-led campaign to free slaves called Loose Change to Loose Chains.[14] Our efforts, however small, can make a difference. As Gary Haugen says, "If God can work through a scrawny little boy who didn't really know how to dress for battle, He can work through simple folks like you and me" (1999:174).

---

14   https://loosechange2loosenchainsatilcs.weebly.com/

CONCLUSION

Modern-day slavery is an extreme human rights violation. It is a slippery, persistent and confounding evil, rendering unprecedented misery to millions of people. The biblical mandate is clear, God's laws demand that we actively do justice to defeat this scourge of modern slavery, which is an affront to the God-given dignity of the human person. Christ's love compels us to protect and restore broken lives. The church, mandated to be a prophetic voice of transformation, needs to sound the clarion call to "pledge to do everything in our power, within our faith communities and beyond, to fight against human trafficking and to work for the freedom of those who have been trafficked and enslaved, that their dignity may be restored and they may once again have reason to hope" (CCMalaysia, 2017).

Together, we can build a world without slavery—a world where it is unthinkable to be treated like someone else's property—a world where those who steal other people's freedoms are brought to justice. A world where everyone can walk free![15]

---

15   https://www.walkfree.org/about/. Accessed 27 Nov 2014.

REFERENCES

Al Jazeera. 2016. "Malaysia: Babies for Sale." Retrieved November 10, 2019. (https://www.aljazeera.com/programmes/101east/2016/11/malaysia-babies-sale-161124133921861.html)

Aryal, Nirmal, Pramod R. Regmi, Erwin Martinez Faller, Edwin van Teijlingen, Chan Chee Khoon, Adrian Pereira, and Padam Simkhada. 2019. "Sudden Cardiac Death and Kidney Health Related Problems Among Nepali Migrant Workers in Malaysia." *Nepali Journal of Epidemiology.* Retrieved November 23, 2019. (https://www.nepjol.info/index.php/NJE/article/view/25805/21541.)

Balasegaram, Mangai. "Human Writes, One Nepali Migrant Worker Died Every Day in Malaysia in 2018." Retrieved March 5, 2020. (https://www.thestar.com.my/lifestyle/living/2019/02/10/migrant-workers-dying)

Batstone, David. 2007. *Not For Sale: The Return of the Global Slave Trade–and How We Can Fight it.* New York: HarperCollins.

Bradbury, Steve. 2005. "Educating for Compassion & Justice: Tear Australia's Education Strategy." *Journal of Christian Education.* 48(3): 35–45.

Brown, Louise. 2000. *Sex Slaves–the Trafficking of Women in Asia.* London, UK: Virago Press.

Catholic Leader. 2009. "Religious Items Produced by Child Slaves." Retrieved November 23, 2019. (https://catholicleader.com.au/news/religious-items-produced-by-child-slaves_52527)

CCMalaysia. 2017. "Interfaith Joint Declaration Against Human Trafficking 30th July 2017." Retrieved November 22, 2019. (http://ccmalaysia.org/index.php/2017/07/interfaith-joint-declaration-against-human-trafficking-30th-july-2017/)

Crouch, Andy. n.d. "The Cruel Edges of the World." Retrieved December 6, 2019. (https://andy-crouch.com/articles/the_cruel_edges_of_the_world)

Fight Slavery Now. n.d. "Products of Labor Abuse." Retrieved November 23, 2014. (https://fightslaverynow.org/why-fight-there-are-27-million-reasons/labortrafficking/products-of-slave-labor/)

George, Abraham. 2014. "Human Trafficking and the Response of the Global Church." *Lausanne Global Analysis* 3(1). Retrieved November 21, 2019. (https://www.lausanne.org/content/lga/2014-01/human-trafficking-and-the-response-of-the-global-church)

Global Slavery Index. 2018. "Country Data—Malaysia." Retrieved November 11, 2019. (https://www.globalslaveryindex.org/2018/data/country-data/malaysia/)

Haugen, Gary A. 1999. *Good News about Injustice: A Witness of Courage in a Hurting World.* Downers Grove, IL: InterVarsity Press.

Home Affairs. 2018. "Commonwealth Modern Slavery Act 2018." Retrieved November 12, 2019. (https://www.homeaffairs.gov.au/criminal-justice/files/modern-slavery-reporting-entities.pdf)

ICAT. 2019. "Human Trafficking and Technology: Trends, Challenges and Opportunities." Issue 7. Retrieved November 11, 2019. (https://phys.org/news/2018-10-link-social-media-sex-trafficking.html)

ILO. 2014. "ILO Says Forced Labour Generates Annual Profits of US$150 Billion." Retrieved November 23, 2019. (https://www.ilo.org/global/about-the-ilo/newsroom/news/WCMS_243201/lang--en/index.htm)

---. 2017. "Forced Labour, Modern Slavery, and Human Trafficking." Retrieved November 11, 2019. (https://www.ilo.org/global/topics/forced-labour/lang--en/index.htm.)

---. n.d. "What is Forced Labour, Modern Slavery, and Human Trafficking?" Retrieved November 11, 2019. (https://www.ilo.org/global/topics/forced-labour/definition/lang--en/index.htm)

Ife, Jim. 2010. *Human Rights From Below: Achieving Rights through Community Development.* Cambridge: Cambridge University Press.

Kahveci, Zeynep Ulku. 2018. "Allow States and Victims to Fight Online Sex Trafficking Act (FOSTA): Senate Passes Bill Making Online Platforms Liable for Third-Party Content Enabling Illegal Sex Trafficking." Retrieved November 11, 2019. (https://jolt.law.harvard.edu/digest/allow-states-and-victims-to-fight-online-sex-trafficking-act-fosta-senate-passes-bill-making-online-platforms-liable-for-third-party-content-enabling-illegal-sex-trafficking)

Keller, Timothy J., 2010. *Generous Justice: How God's Grace Makes Us Just.* New York, NY: Riverhead Books.

Kelly, Annie. 2014. "I Carried His Name on my Body for Nine Years: The Tattooed Trafficking Survivors Reclaiming their Past." Retrieved November 23, 2014.(https://www.theguardian.com/global-development/2014/nov/16/sp-the-tattooed-trafficking-survivors-reclaiming-their-past)

Khidhir, Sheith. 2019. "Human Trafficking Thriving in ASEAN. Retrieved November 12, 2019. (https://theaseanpost.com/article/human-trafficking-thriving-asean)

Kralis, Barbara. 2006. "Catholic Church's Fight Against Trafficking & Human Slavery." Retrieved November 21, 2014. (https://www.catholicculture.org/culture/library/view.cfm?recnum=7106)

Marshall, Christopher D. 2002. *Crowned with Glory and Honor: Human Rights in the Biblical Tradition.* Telford, PA: Pandora.

McLaren, Brian D., Padilla, Elisa, & Seeber, Ashley Bunting, eds. 2009. *The Justice Project.* Grand Rapids, MI: Baker Books.

New Straits Times. 2017. "The Secrets of Wang Kelian Exposed." Retrieved November 12, 2019. (https://www.nst.com.my/news/exclusive/2017/12/316339/exclusive-secrets-wang-kelian-exposed)

Ramachandra, Vinoth. 2008. *Subverting Global Myths: Theology and the Public Issues Shaping Our World.* Downers Grove, IL: InterVarsity Press.

Reliefweb, 2019. "Sold Like Fish": Crimes Against Humanity, Mass Graves, and Human Trafficking from Myanmar and Bangladesh to Malaysia from 2012 to 2015." Retrieved November 21, 2019. (https://reliefweb.int/report/malaysia/sold-fish-crimes-against-humanity-mass-graves-and-human-trafficking-myanmar-and)

Skinner, E. Benjamin. 2008. *A Crime so Monstrous: Face-to-Face with Modern-Day Slavery.* New York: First Free Press.

Sloane, Andrew. 2011. *Justifying Advocacy: A Biblical and Theological Rationale for Speaking the Truth to Power on Behalf of the Vulnerable.* The John Saunders Lecture. http://www.ethos.org.au/online-resources/blog/justifying-advocacy---speaking-truth-to-power

Suhakam. 2004. *Trafficking in Women and Children: Report of the Human Rights Commission of Malaysia (SUHAKAM).* Kuala Lumpur, Malaysia. https://www.suhakam.org.my/wp-content/uploads/2013/12/Trafficking-in-women-and-children2004.pdf

Tenaganita, 2009. *The Global Catch: Modern Day Slavery Fishermen.* Published by Tenaganita Sdn Bhd, Kuala Lumpur, Malaysia.

---. 2016a. "Sex Workers Treated Like Baby Factories." Retrieved November, 11, 2019. (http://www.tenaganita.net/news-and-press-releases/press-releases/sex-workers-treated-like-baby-factories/)

---. 2016b. "In Malaysia, 128,000 People Effectively Slaves, Survey Finds." Retrieved November 21, 2019. (http://www.tenaganita.net/news-and-press-releases/news/in-malaysia-128800-people-effectively-slaves-survey-finds/)

---. 2018. "Joint Press Statement by Tenaganita & Change Your World: Fight Human Trafficking through BE MY PROTECTOR App." Retrieved November 12, 2019. (http://www.tenaganita.net/news-and-press-releases/press-releases/joint-press-statement-by-tenaganita-change-your-world-fight-human-trafficking-through-be-my-protector-app/)

---. 2019. "Child Sex Trade Growing in Malaysia, Tenaganita Warns." Retrieved November 21, 2019. (http://www.tenaganita.net/news-and-press-releases/news/child-sex-trade-growing-in-malaysia-tenaganita-warns/)

---. n.d. "Anti Trafficking in Persons." Retrieved November 21, 2014. (http://www.tenaganita.net/our-work/anti-trafficking-in-persons/)

Tham, Jia Vern. 2018. "Malaysian NGOs Launched the First Ever Anti-Human Trafficking App in Southeast Asia." Retrieved November 12, 2019. (https://says.com/my/tech/malaysian-ngos-launched-the-first-ever-anti-human-trafficking-app-in-southeast-asia)

The Cape Town Commitment. 2011. *A Confession of Faith and a Call to Action.* A Resource from the Lausanne Movement. Malaysia : Thumbprints Utd.

The Straits Times. 2014. "Modern Slavery Affects 35.8 Million People Worldwide: Report." Retrieved March 5, 2020. (https://www.straitstimes.com/world/europe/modern-slavery-affects-358-million-people-worldwide-report)

True Story Award. n.d. "Winners." Retrieved November 12, 2019. (https://truestoryaward.org/winners)

United Nations, n.d. "First Decade of the Mandate of the Special Rapporteur on Trafficking in Persons, Especially Women and Children." Retrieved November 21, 2019. (https://www.ohchr.org/Documents/Issues/Trafficking/FirsDecadeSRon_%20trafficking.pdf)

University of Toledo. 2018. "Study Details Link between Social Media and Sex Trafficking." Retrieved on November 11, 2019. (https://phys.org/news/2018-10-link-social-media-sex-trafficking.html)

UNODC. 2020. "Human Trafficking." Retrieved March 5, 2020. (https://www.unodc.org/unodc/en/human-trafficking/what-is-human-trafficking.html#What_is_Human_Trafficking)

US Embassy. 2019. "2019 Trafficking Report in Malaysia." Retrieved November 21, 2019. (https://my.usembassy.gov/our-relationship/official-reports/report-2019-trafficking-in-persons-062019/)

Villa, Monique. 2018. "Why Business is the Best Partner in the Fight Against Modern Slavery." Retrieved November 21, 2019. (https://www.weforum.org/agenda/2018/01/businesses-are-the-best-partners-in-the-fight-against-modern-slavery/)

WEA. 2020. "Exposed: Shining a Light on Corruption." Retrieved November 22, 2019. (http://www.worldevangelicals.org/exposed/#.XmB69OczbSZ)

Wink, Walter. 1998. *The Powers That Be: Theology for a New Millennium.* New York, NY: Doubleday.

Wolterstorff, Nicholas. 2013. *Journey Towards Justice: Personal Encounters in the Global South.* Grand Rapids, MI: Baker Academic.

Wright, Christopher. J. H. 2004. *Old Testament Ethics for the People of God.* Leicester, England: Inter-Varsity Press.

Yee, Elroi, Ian Yee, Lim May Lee and Samantha Chow. n.d. "Inside the Student Trafficking Trade."
    Retrieved November 12, 2019. (https://www.rage.com.my/student-trafficking-trade/
    #3GtF8ySpxz8uOGJe.99)

WOMEN AND MIGRATION IN CAMBODIA: A STUDY IN GENDER INEQUALITY OR EMPOWERMENT?

Karen Lim

INTRODUCTION

Cambodia is a land of contradictions. It conjures up images of Angkor Wat and the Khmer Rouge from its long ago and more recent history. But today, images of monks in saffron robes, ornate temples, rice fields and smiling children are also juxtaposed with sweat shops, child trafficking and sex workers.

A nation rebuilding itself after a war that will always mark its history and legacy. Cambodia, currently in the process of changing and recreating itself, is no exception. Bustling streets, colourful markets, traffic congestion, and never-sleeping street commerce reflect a country that has moved from a closed socialist economy to one driven by the markets.

The people, too, are changing as they negotiate new opportunities against the constraints of tradition. Predominantly rural rice people, a new generation of Cambodians is seeking ways to participate in the prosperity and development of the country. For them, Phnom Penh conjures up images of lights and activity where people have jobs, wear nice clothes, and *daeleng* (which literally translates as "walking for leisure", meaning "having fun"). Modernisation, migration and urbanisation are significant phenomena in Cambodian society today.

Cambodian women have played an important part in the changing landscape. Economic growth in Cambodia in the last two decades has been fuelled by women-dominated growth engines—the garment industry and tourism being two key contributors. Migrant women have commonly been portrayed as unwilling subjects of exploitation (low wages, poor working conditions and abuse), forced to work under conditions that entrench gender inequalities, and even lead to increasing gender-based violence. Without dismissing the fact that economic conditions, structural inequalities and cultural constructs have had a negative impact on migrant women, this depiction of their plight is not the only story. They are also agents in the constant economic and social reconstruction of Cambodia. In fact, urbanisation and migration are even contributing to the empowerment of Cambodian women (Derks, 2008:198–206).

This chapter will examine traditional and cultural constraints for women's participation in the economic, political and social dimensions of Cambodian society, as well as the changes that have taken place in recent years. It will analyse the causes and impacts of these changes on Cambodian women, with a particular focus on women who have migrated to work in the garment factories.

UNDERSTANDING GENDER IN THE CAMBODIAN CONTEXT

Understanding gender in Cambodia involves reconciling contradictory and seemingly incompatible realities. Women are perceived as subservient to male dominance, yet much evidence also points to the relative equality of men and women.

Women have played an eminent role in Khmer culture. Queens Indradevi and Jayarajadevi encouraged education, public healthcare, and spirituality during the glorious Angkorian empire, which influenced the South-east Asian region between the ninth and thirteenth centuries. Angkor Wat, the pride of Cambodia, is filled with intricate carvings of Apsara goddesses that embodied purity, virtue, femininity and strength.

Cambodian women have fairly equal standing in a household. They participate in economic activity, have a decisive role in decision-making, and even exercise control over household expenses. Traditionally, women plant rice in the paddy fields alongside their husbands and are also diligent in small entrepreneurial activities to earn extra income for the family.

Cambodian women traditionally have relatively high status because of the bilateral kinship system that allows a woman to maintain lineage to her family. Unlike women of Chinese or Indian ancestry, baby girls are preferred to baby boys. Bride wealth is paid, married couples often live with or near the bride's family, and inheritance is divided between sons and daughters. A daughter is also more likely to care for her ageing parents in their old age, a demonstration of filial piety that is valued in Cambodian culture.

Foreign powers, the Khmer Rouge war, and changing societal traditions have impacted gender equality. The Siamese invasion of the Angkorian empire, and the encroachment of the Vietnamese and French colonial powers, have all contributed to the destruction of Khmer culture and traditions that were anchored in the golden age of an educated and proud people. This decimation intensified under the Khmer Rouge, which systematically sought to eradicate the remaining cultural vestiges of a once proud people. Today, Cambodia is one of the poorest countries in the region, with very little to offer apart from tourism built on both its recent grim history and its once glorious past.

Women are central to the rebuilding of the nation, providing the skilled workforce for the garment industry—the key driver of the nation's economy. Thus, they are in the middle of the huge change resulting from modernisation and urbanisation, and must navigate this rapidly changing cultural landscape.

HIERARCHICAL NATURE OF CAMBODIA'S SOCIAL ORDER

Any discussion on roles and gender requires the reader to understand the hierarchical nature of Cambodian society. This is clearly reflected even in the language, where words differentiate between the status of each speaker.

Status and honour are accorded based on a variety of factors, such as wealth, familial connection, marital status, age, religious piety, employment and, especially, gender. The concept of status is rooted in the Buddhist belief of merit and *karma*. Buddhists believe that one's status today is linked to the activities of one's past life, and what one does today will affect one's next life.

Men gain merit when they become monks, whilst women gain merit as donors: feeding monks, donating wealth and their sons (as monks) to the pagoda (Ledgerwood, Judy and Vijghen, John, 1990:36–37). Men are spiritual whereas women are caught up with worldliness, thus making them inferior. Age is the other important marker of status. Respect for elders is very important in Cambodian culture. An older woman may in the latter years of her life gain merit through participation in Buddhist ceremonies. Grandmothers often crop their hair short to symbolise their renunciation of preoccupation with worldly tasks once so central in their younger lives.

This social order may seem determined by a higher moral order (Ledgerwood, *Women in Cambodian Society*, n.d.), but it serves to legitimise power within the current hierarchy—even when power is abused. In other words, it reinforces the status quo. In a market economy driven by greed, corroding moral codes and a sense of self-earned entitlement, those who "have" feel they have gotten what they deserve. The "have-nots" are not seen as victims of systemic injustice but people deserving of their ill-fate, either because of laziness or fate as assigned by *karma*.

I was once told that I must have done something good in my past life to deserve such a loving and caring husband. The tragedy is that the reverse is also thought to be true: it is common for a Cambodian woman to take responsibility for the abuse she receives from her husband, as it is assumed that bad karma from her previous life had led to the abuse!

Fifty percent of women versus 27 percent of men aged 15–49 believed that a husband was justified in beating his wife if she has argued with him, neglected the children, refused sex, left the house without his permission, or even burned food (*2014 Cambodia Demographic and Health Survey*,

2014). These statistics reveal women's poor understanding of their rights. An educated woman is more likely to be aware of her rights and challenge abuse. Domestic violence correlates to poverty, as financial stress and desperation stimulate violence. Alcohol is often cited as a contributing factor.

Although still practiced, the bilateral kinship system is corroding. Whilst before, a girl was likely to remain living with her parents until marriage, many girls now leave their parent's home at an earlier age as they migrate to the city for work or studies. Also, whereas once arranged marriages were the norm, today's parents have less influence over their child's choice of spouse. These factors may contribute to higher levels of spousal abuse against women as they leave the protection of their families.

A person's honour or status is very much linked to how a family views an individual or how the wider community views a family. Honour and status are not static, and can be earned through proper "codes of conduct", or preserved through efforts to "save face". Preservation of a family's honour and status is ingrained in Cambodian culture and every person carries this responsibility (and burden) from the time they are old enough to understand.

When power and status conditions social and gender roles, the hierarchical order becomes a constraint to development and gender equality. Cultural expectations of daughters are encoded in the *Chbap Srey* or *Rules of the Lady*, a widely accepted code of conduct for Cambodian women. It is strongly accepted that a woman's place in the social order depends on her ability to fulfil these rules. A woman who behaves "properly", i.e. in alignment with this code, is accorded high status (Ledgerwood and Vijghen, 1990.) "To be an improper woman is to cease to be Khmer, and given Khmer notions of the centrality of Khmerness, to cease to be Khmer is to cease to be fully human," writes Judy Ledgerwood (Chey, n.d.).

In order to better understand the *Chbap Srey*, I sought help from two colleagues—Savy and Eth, both well-educated adult women. My questions were met with giggles and shy smiles. I did not have to prod much before they launched into the rules.

"We must take the smallest and gentlest steps. Nobody must hear even the rustle of our sarongs." — *Kim, Savy*

"A married woman can give advice to her husband but she must also be the servant in the house." — *May, Eth*

"We must work hard. A good wife must be industrious!" — *Kim, Savy*

"A woman must talk softly so as not to shame her husband when she speaks. Especially if one lives in a wooden house." — *May, Eth*

"Unmarried women must be demure and protected by their relatives." — *May, Eth*

The *Chbap Srey* touches on many aspects of how a proper, respectable woman should look and behave in Cambodian society: how to walk, how to speak, how to dress, what work a woman should or should not do, her restricted role in society. Both Savy and Eth learnt the *Chbap Srey* in primary school as part of their official curriculum and at home from their mothers.

Savy saw the *Chbap Srey* as something positive, and an integral part of her identity as a lady. It gave her confidence because she was acknowledged by men and family. *Chbap Srey* provided laws that protected her honour as well as the honour of her family.

Eth said the rules led to gender discrimination, as girls were traditionally not allowed to get an education as learning was a risk to the rules and may lead to misbehaviour.

It fascinated me that the rules highlighted by my "modern", educated colleagues were those that referred to servitude to husband and family, submission and seeking approval from men. I had expected that modernisation and an education would have accorded them a stronger sense of self, independence and value as women.

Although the rules may change with age and marital status, the *Chbap Srey* puts contradicting demands on women. A woman's behaviour affects the status of her husband, father, and even sons. She has the power, on one hand, to upset the entire social structure through how she behaves, but, on the other, she is a slave to this expectation. Khmer women are to be soft-spoken, gentle and yet industrious and strong. Women are the servants at home but often have real control of finances. As Ledgerwood so astutely remarks, "Women are supposed to be many things, the dominating woman who is competent in the marketplace and in the fields, and the woman who defers to her husband in all public conversations" (*Women in Cambodian Society*, n.d.). In recent decades, even though unmarried girls are traditionally required to be protected and kept at home, many have been sent to Phnom Penh to earn money.

These contradictory ideals and changing meanings have allowed Cambodian women to navigate modernity whilst holding to their gender ideals. However, balancing their lives with the social order and expectations of the *Chbap Srey* is not a recent need. For generations, Cambodian women have learnt to adapt their qualities and ideals according to different situations and navigated the ambiguity of ideals with the demands of reality.

The Role of Recent History: The Unwanted Legacy of the Khmer Rouge

For decades, Cambodians have been a people on the move. The Khmer Rouge regime's civil violence saw a mass exodus of people out of Phnom Penh and the utter destruction of Cambodia's social capital. Families were separated and children were taken away into separate camps, some training as soldiers.

An estimated two million Cambodians died during the war in the 1970s from starvation, disease, war and executions. When the war ended, Cambodia's adult female population was significantly higher than that of the men. Some cite a 64 percent representation of women in the adult population in the early 1990s with 35 percent of households headed by women (Ledgerwood, *Women in Cambodian Society* (n.d)). More women survived the war because they were less likely to be connected to the old regime or seen as a threat by the Khmer Rouge. They were also driven by the need to care for their children and were better able to survive malnutrition (Ebihara and Ledgerwood, 2002:272–291). After the end of the Khmer Rouge war, many more men were killed or maimed in the on-going civil war. Studies have found higher mortality rates amongst men aged 15–34 in the civil war period 1975–79, a high indication of violent death (Walque, 2004:5–6).

When peace finally came to the nation after the Paris Peace Agreement in 1991, the Cambodian people were left with the task of rebuilding the economy of their war-ravaged country, replacing lost human capital, and restoring the Khmer cultural heritage.

With the absence of men, women took on many of the roles previously undertaken by men. In rural areas, they farmed the fields and cultivated new land; in the urban spaces, they took on administrative roles previously occupied by the educated men.

The composition of households, and the social relationships within, then changed after the war due to demographic imbalances. There was a surplus of women, leading literally to their devaluation. Moreover, the many female-headed households were more likely to struggle with daily survival than those in which there was both a wife and husband (Ebihara and Ledgerwood, 2002:272–291).

The socio-demographic changes forced women again to navigate between the perceived ideal and necessity. The traditional and cultural constraints that had shaped Cambodian women's participation in the workforce, politics and society were loosened by the war, and post-war Cambodia allowed space for women to take part in the reconstruction of the nation. Indeed, they were needed.

DEMOGRAPHIC CHANGES SINCE THE WAR

The post-war "baby boom" resulted in the young median age of Cambodia's population (Vachon, 2017). In 2008, 65.3 percent of the population were

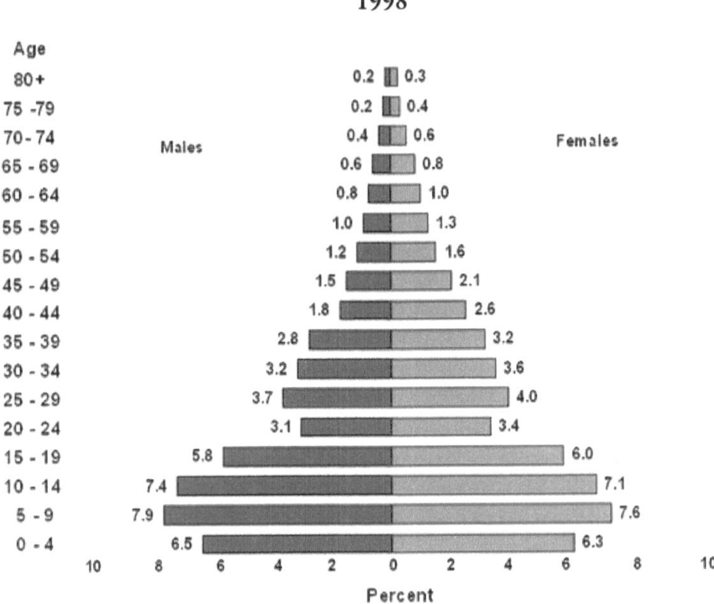

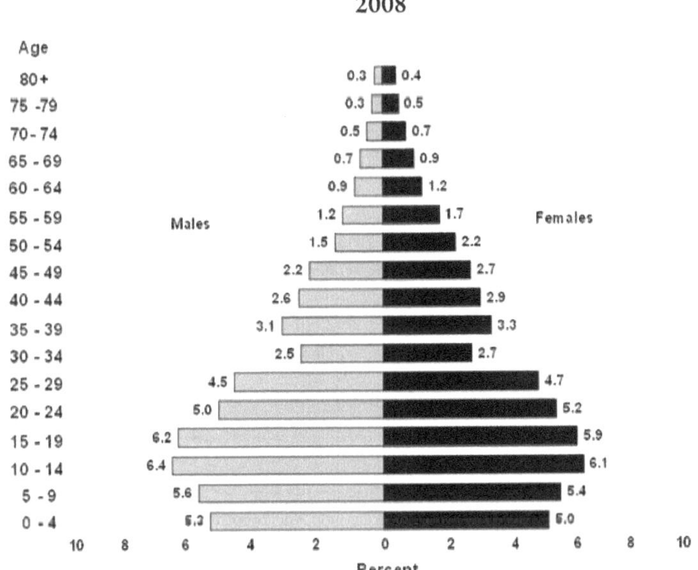

Figure 1. Age pyramids of Cambodia 2008 vs 1998
(General Population Census of Cambodia 2008, 2009)

under the age of 30 (*General Population Census of Cambodia 2008, 2009*).

The baby boomer surge provided Cambodia with an opportunity to reap a demographic dividend. But this cohort was predominantly poorly educated and low-skilled due to the slow rebuilding of the country's education system.

The main engines of economic growth in Cambodia—garments, construction and tourism—have absorbed much of this labour force during the last two decades, providing employment for a new generation of female waged labour. The garment industry in Cambodia has been highlighted for exploitative practices. International attention has put pressure both on the buyers and the producers, resulting in positive efforts to improve working conditions and increase the minimum wages of factory workers. Cambodia's loss of least-developed country (LDC) status in 2015, together with the expected withdrawal of preferential trade privileges, is expected to decrease the competitiveness of Cambodian garments. Indeed, foreign investment has already decreased, which could result in many women losing their jobs in the coming years and becoming susceptible to other forms of exploitative labour. An example is debt bondage by brick-kiln owners, recently highlighted as an exploitative industry that has gone under-radar as construction booms in the country. Another would be the sex and entertainment industry boosted by increased tourism from China.

The age dependency ratio[1] in 2016 was 55.4 percent (*World Bank: Age Dependency Ratio*, 2016). This means that for every 100 working-age persons there will be 55.4 dependents. In Malaysia, the ratio is 45 percent and in Thailand 40 percent. As Cambodia moves from a young to intermediate population, the coming generation needs to be better educated, better skilled, and equipped to enter the workforce with the skills and knowledge that will secure them work in the civil service or private sector. The burden of caring for the elderly is culturally the responsibility of daughters. For women to adequately care for the elderly

---

1   Definition: Age dependency ratio is the ratio of dependents (people younger than 15 or older than 64) to the working-age population (those between the ages of 15 and 64). The data shows the proportion of dependents per 100 working-age population.

in the next generation, today's girls must be accorded the opportunities to gain knowledge and the right marketable skills that will enable them to get better jobs and earn a decent income.

MIGRATION IN CAMBODIA

Cambodians continue to move to the larger centre and the urban population is growing. Women are a big part of this exodus. As the country develops and opens up to the global economy, attitudes to entrepreneurship and risks have changed. Availability to finance allows for new possibilities and opportunities. The social construct of a country determines access to these opportunities depending on power, willingness to take on different types of labour, and need.

Cambodia has sustained an average GDP growth of 7.6 percent in 1994–2015 and registered 6.9 percent in 2016 (*World Bank*, 2017). Growth has been limited to the three main growth engines of garments, tourism and construction. This has led to increased migration to urban areas, especially Phnom Penh, where much of the work around these sectors are concentrated. Phnom Penh has more than doubled between the 1998 and 2008 census periods (Zimmer, 2012).

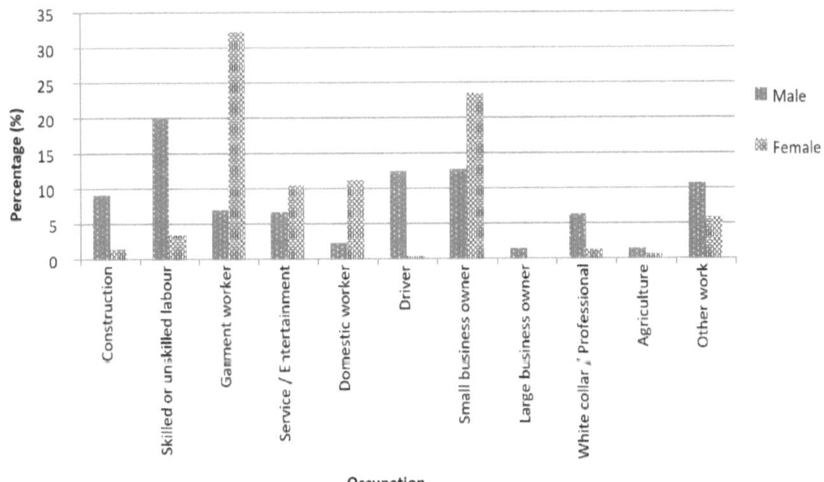

Figure 2. Occupations taken by migrants to Phnom Penh (They, Kheam & Emily Treleaven, 2013:6)

In a survey done of a sample in 2013, 56.9 percent of migrants to Phnom Penh were women, with concentrated primary occupations as garment worker (32.2%), small-business owner (23.4%), domestic worker (11.1%), and service/entertainment worker (10.3%) (They & Treleaven, 2013, 6). Although the garment industry is showing signs of slowing down due to decreased competitiveness, garments still contributed to 67 percent of Cambodia's exports in the first half of 2017 compared to 75 percent in the same period last year (Manet, 2017).

Care Australia estimates that 600,000 are working in the garment industry with 85 percent of those employed being women, of which 66 percent are under the age of 30 (*SHCS Brief: Women in Cambodia's Garment Industry*, 2016).

Reasons for migration can be understood in many ways. It is necessary to realise that reasons are interlinked and decisions are often based on a combination of factors.

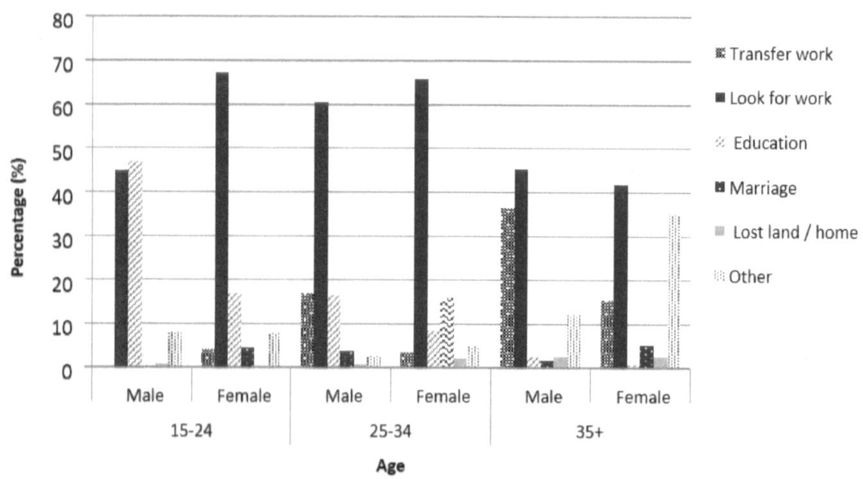

Figure 3. Motivation for moving by sex and age
(They, Kheam & Emily Treleaven, 2013:5)

Individual Decisions Based on "Push" and "Pull" Factors

> "Look around! We are only old people here. Our young people leave to find work." — *Villager in Kampong Speu*

> "I love my village! If there are jobs here, I will not leave it. But now with the drought I need to leave and find work in the city." — *Youth in Kampot*

Greater employment opportunities—with higher wages and better working conditions—are attracting large numbers into cities like Phnom Penh. It is the cities that are the engines of economic growth in Cambodia, and young internal migrants are being attracted to them in large numbers. The Cambodian census in 2008 revealed, for example, that only 30 percent of the population in Phnom Penh were born there (Planning, 2012:7).

In rural Cambodia, poor land management and land grabbing have caused an increase in the numbers of landless people. This, together with the impact of climate change, has led to a decline in agricultural productivity and further economic hardship in rural communities. Demographic pressures due to the bulging workforce are also forcing working-age adults to migrate to the urban areas, and across borders to neighbouring countries, in the search for new livelihoods.

Household Strategy

Theories of migration that focus on individual decision-making are too narrow for the current reality (Zimmer, 2012:4). Decisions to migrate in Cambodia is rarely an individual decision—migration is a household strategy for survival. Remittances are an important factor in a decision to leave one's family to find work. The garment industry is an essential source of remittance to the countryside, which has an important anti-poverty effect with an estimated 1 million Cambodians benefiting directly from remittances (*ILO, Women and Work in the Garment Factory*, 2006:4). Care Australia reports that garment workers send home an average of 40 percent of their salary.

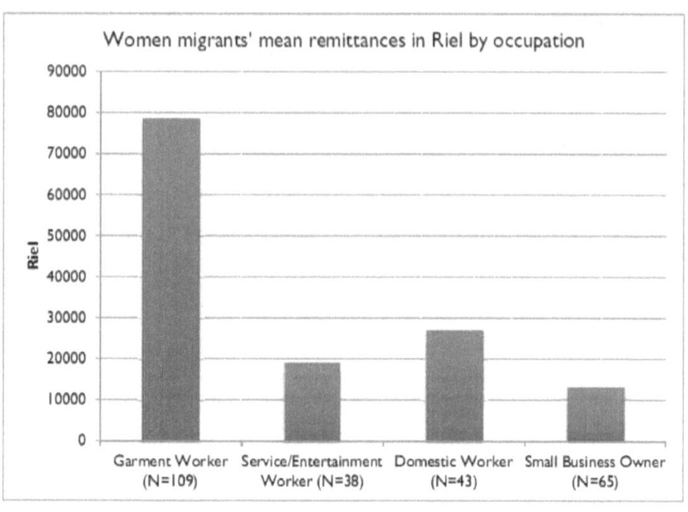

Figure 4. Mean remittances per month by occupation
(They, Kheam & Emily Treleaven, 2013:17)

Network

Studies have found that family and village relationships play a critical role in rural-urban migration. Social ties, the *ksae* (literally translates as "string", meaning a "connection or contact") (Derks, 2008:35) link a migrant to their place of origin and the destination. This may be a family member or a fellow villager that has already migrated, developed a social network in Phnom Penh, and is now mediating the migration process for others. They may help village women find jobs or provide a place to stay in the place of destination. Peers play an important role influencing which sector of work a migrant woman enters. The *ksae* eases the many uncertainties associated with migration. Parents are put at ease as to the dangers of migration, such as sexual exploitation and security.

Modernisation has enhanced the ability to network. Mobile phones are found everywhere, amongst the very poor, and in the remotest of places. This has not only helped families cope with separation but also brings the influences of urban living closer to village life. In my visits to rural families, it is quite common to see phone numbers scrawled on walls and wooden beams of a house.

Structural Conditions

As Cambodia shifts from a closed socialist economy to one driven by the market, money becomes the main driver of purchase, need, and want. Where before subsistence living was the norm of the rural majority, people are now forced to do anything or sell anything to survive. Slavery as previously understood may not exist, but the question of how much disadvantaged women are willing to compromise to access the needed economic sphere is a critical question of rights and justice.

Neoliberal restructuring has often been criticised for worsening the socio-demographic status of women in much of the global south (Grez, n.d.). As investments are made in areas with the most monetary gains, there are increasing cutbacks on social needs like healthcare and education. Women, especially female-headed households with already limited survival strategies, are left vulnerable and forced to migrate from their homes in the rural areas to the cities where the work is—even at the risk of safety and health.

Renowned sociologist Saskia Sassen has shown the link between globalisation and the migration of third-world women both within their country and abroad. Waged labour has been feminised as factories are moved to low-cost developing countries, enabling capitalists to increase profits through a low-waged, easily controlled, and therefore easily exploited workforce (Sassen, 1984). Women are less likely to fight bad working conditions and are willing to work for less. An explanation for this could be that in many third-world cultures women may traditionally have been seen as submissive and not supposed to stand up against men. To change this will take time.

There are stories of factories that closed down overnight without paying the staff their fair share. Poor ventilation in crowded areas causes mass faintings, and should a worker fall sick there will be cuts in the salary. Labour unions are still somewhat restricted, and a vast supply of unemployed workers means that if you are unhappy with your working conditions there will be many who are ready to take your place. Women who have migrated into the cities are at the mercy of the factory owners.

Personal Desire and Motivation

Cambodian society, despite its poverty, is becoming increasingly materialistic. Media and television play a big role in communicating the allures of modern city life. Girls dream of being a city girl instead of a village girl.

Material gain and a free modern lifestyle are all attractive notions for a sheltered village girl. She desires freedom and Phnom Penh offers it. Friends come back with nice clothes, jewellery, make up—all the material things many girls desire. The city is a place of escape from the constraints and difficulties faced in the village—control by parents, spousal abuse, and hard labour on the farm.

A girl's reasons for urban living may change with time, as she navigates through both gender ideals and material desire. A girl may leave at first to earn money for her household and, in spite of many heart-warming stories of women sacrificing for family, there are those who use their money to satisfy their aspirations for consumption. Some women move to the big, dangerous city despite the opposition of family, and in these cases can become alienated from the family.

Rural-urban migration illuminates "both how social relations of domination and exploitation are reproduced as well as how they are negotiated, contested and reworked in individual experience" (Mills, 1999:5). Women cleverly navigate through gender constructs as they "shift between various positions in their interactions with their rural home, urban work, and with their peers, including the opposite sex" (Derks, 2008:58).

THE IMPACTS OF URBANISATION, MIGRATION AND MODERNISATION IN CAMBODIA

Growing Social and Economic Inequality

In 2009 Cambodia achieved the Millennium Development Goal (MDG) target of halving poverty rates. Although the poverty rate in 2014 was 13.5 percent, compared to 47.8 percent in 2007 (*World Bank*, 2017), the majority of those who escaped poverty managed to do so only by a small margin. Four-and-a-half million near-poor teeter just above the poverty line and are extremely vulnerable to economic shocks that could quickly push them back below it.

High GDP growth masks inequality, abuse, and exploitation. Development in Cambodia has not been inclusive, and the country suffers from poor resource management, pro-rich land management, and a lack of good governance. Those with power and wealth wield the most political and economic power, allowing them to make even more money. Widespread corruption is the accepted norm, putting those unable to bribe at a disadvantage. Growing crime is not uncommon, as people find all ways possible to acquire money. Social benefits are withheld to wield power over the working class. Ecological degradation worsens as it costs money to ensure clean air and water. The working class is constantly threatened with unrest, instability and loss of their livelihoods should they fight the "system".

There is evidence that gender affects the poverty experience. Women are less likely to have the resources to cope with poverty, more likely to be caught in unpaid hard domestic work. Women are more likely to be the first to go hungry and the least likely to be given access to education to get themselves out of the cycle of poverty (*In Focus: Women & Poverty, UN Women*, n.d.). Declines in poverty rates do not necessarily translate to equal access to resources within a household. High incidences of malnutrition among women and incidences of domestic violence indicate the inferior position assigned to women. Households headed by women are also especially vulnerable to shocks due to social and cultural constraints, limited economic opportunities and lower land-holding. The Gender Inequality Index (GII)[2] gives an illustration of how this looks like across countries. The higher the GII value, the more the disparities between females and males. Cambodia has a GII of 0.479 compared to 0.366 in Thailand and 0.203 in the USA (UNDP, 2016).

---

2   Gender Inequality Index (GII): A composite measure reflecting inequality in achievement between women and men in three dimensions: reproductive health, empowerment, and the labour market.

Gender Disparities in the Labour Market

De jure recognition of the Convention for the Elimination of all forms of Discrimination Against Women (CEDAW)[3] by the Cambodian government has not translated into the elimination of discrimination of Cambodian women. Rural women with low literacy and education are not aware of their rights, which is why some NGOs in Cambodia are working to establish grassroot networks of women's groups that will raise awareness of rights and reduce widespread discrimination.

The mean years of education received by people ages 25 and older is only 3.7 years for girls compared to 5.5 years for boys. The gap is larger when looking at secondary education with only 13.2 percent of females aged 25 years and older with at least some secondary education versus 26.1 percent of males (UNDP, 2016).

Gender gaps in participation and employment rates have only declined marginally, with young women facing the highest risk of unemployment. Although labour force participation[4] for females has increased—75.5 percent vs 86.7 percent for males (UNDP, 2016)—women are disproportionately employed in low-wage activities with 75 percent of working women in agriculture (*ADB, Cambodia needs more support to achieve its gender equality goals*, 2017).

Even though in recent years women have played an integral part in the labour market, and laws[5] stipulate that women have equality in all spheres of employment, there is still much to be done to reduce gender inequalities at work. Women are not equally remunerated, and social benefits are not

---

3   For the purposes of the present Convention, the term "discrimination against women" shall mean any distinction, exclusion, or restriction made on the basis of sex which has the effect or purpose of impairing or nullifying the recognition, enjoyment, or exercise by women, irrespective or their marital status, on a basis of equality of men and women, of human rights and fundamental freedoms in the political, economic, social, cultural, civil, or any other field. — Article 1, CEDAW.

4   Proportion of the working-age population (ages 15 and older) that engages in the labour market, either by working or actively looking for work, expressed as a percentage of the working-age population. Source: ILO (2016b). ILOSTAT database. http://www.ilo.org/ilostat. Accessed 24 October 2016.

5   Article 36 of the Constitution and Articles 172 to 188 pertaining to Cambodian labour laws.

provided to women. The many women employed informally in the entertainment industry and small-scale trading enterprises, or as domestic helpers or waitresses, are particularly vulnerable, as even the most rudimentary benefits are hard to enforce in those sectors.

Care Australia found that the average basic salary in 2015 of female workers in the garment industry was USD145 per month, compared to USD161 for male workers. Despite women dominating the industry, supervisory and management roles are often held by men. Only 4 percent of women in the industry hold positions of leadership, either as a line leader or office worker (*SHCS Brief: Women in Cambodia's Garment Industry*, 2016).

Factory owners have often acted with impunity, flouting rules and regulations not only regarding wages but also basic safety/health standards, knowing that those who oppose can be easily replaced. Some garment workers have resorted to providing sex for supplementary income.

Health issues disproportionately affect women migrants. Garment workers often minimise their own spending to send more money home. They are likely to deprive themselves of their own subsistence, work long hours overtime, and compromise healthcare. Care Australia's report states that one out of three women is experiencing sexual harassment. Despite this high number, women still go to work as taking time off reduces their income (Dr Lawreniuk and Parsons, 2016). There has also been a growing concern about increased prevalence of HIV/AIDS among women as a result of the growing entertainment/sex industry.

Impact on Households Left Behind

Khmer women are industrious. They have traditionally worked alongside their husbands in the rice fields and cared for their families with extreme diligence. Women are the first up in the wee hours to clean the house, wash laundry and prepare food for their still sleeping family. Rural women will wake up extra early to do these chores before heading out to the fields. This double duty of both housework and paid labour is not uncommon all around the world, especially in agricultural-based societies. Statistics show that girls stop their education at primary school if they are needed to help in household chores or take on the day-to-day running of their household when their mother migrates for work.

Women are more conscious than men of the economic hardships back home, and desire to alleviate the hardships faced by the families they have left behind even as they have taken up employment elsewhere. Children may be neglected by those who are supposed to care for them. Villages are emptied of their able-bodied men and working-aged women, leaving neglect in the farms and village households. We often find only the very old and the young remaining in the village.

Changing Gender Norms

Gender relations in Cambodia are changing. Women have emerged as a great economic power and the constraints of the *Chbap Srey* are being challenged and breached as Cambodia goes through economic, social and political development.

Cambodian women have not only taken over some roles traditionally seen as male-dominated, but stimulated some of the key growth engines of the Cambodian economy. When asked, a villager said that the one thing that has changed Cambodian society the past decade is the women-dominated garment industry. The influx of foreign visitors due to tourism as well as local visitors have also seen a rise in the entertainment/sex industry. Women have always engaged in small trading, and are always creatively finding ways to increase household income. Oftentimes they earn more money for the family than their husbands, especially if the latter continue in more traditional livelihoods in the countryside, such as subsistence farming.

Development has been perceived to bring about more empowerment opportunities for women than men. Women are more mobile than ever before, have gained control over finances, resulting in a rise of their confidence and self-esteem. But this has also led to some reports of marital conflicts and a rise in domestic violence.

Conflicting ideals of Khmer gender roles allow women to adapt with time and need and justify new patterns of behaviour (Ledgerwood, 1994:119–128). Whilst unmarried girls are expected to be protected at home, market demands have created employment opportunities for young girls. A girl leaving her village and living unsupervised could be a topic for gossip, but a girl is expected to support her family. Families are suddenly having to grapple with these new conflicting tensions. Whilst maintaining that a family's honour linked to unmarried daughters is important, the hard economic realities of poverty and the need to feed their families become stronger drivers of decisions than traditional social norms.

ADAPTATION OF THE GARMENT WORKER

In the popular song "The Weeping of the Garment Factory Worker" (Derks, 2008:70), we hear the story of a girl who became a garment factory worker to earn money to support herself. She is now filled with regret, but can find no way out of her predicament. While there is truth in the song, it paints a rather one-sided picture of the situation faced by young garment workers. There are certainly hardships and challenges, but not everything is negative. Many have escaped the hardships of rice planting and found the excitement of city living. They may also have escaped what they experienced as the suffocating control of parents and the constraints of tradition. They have had to adapt to new forms of labour discipline but they have also gained independence and freedom. Moving is dependent on connections and networks both for housing and work, but these networks also provide the social and security support for young girls. Factory work allows them to work in the shade rather than labouring under the hot sun and developing "dark" skin (Cambodian women equate fair skin with beauty). However, hierarchies exist in the factories, and the girls are often supervised by Chinese who have different ideas about management and discipline.

The garment industry for all its vices and inequalities has provided rural women the opportunity to be part of the social, economic and even political development of this country. Despite the inequalities and challenges, many female garment workers have learnt how to deal with *the evil bosses* mentioned in the song.

Previously garment workers were reluctant to fight for better wages and work conditions. Their earnings were good compared to other jobs. They also felt they had limited bargaining positions as they were easily replaceable. Lack of knowledge about the labour law and their perceived inferior position in the social order prevented them from fighting work-place injustice. In recent years, however, the industry has become increasingly unionised. Women have become more aware of their rights and have demanded better wages and work conditions. Moreover, factories are aware that open resistance will inevitably affect profitability and draw criticism, and could result in the withdrawal of buyers. Big international fast fashion labels like H&M, MANGO, and Zara have all been pressured by negative international publicities surrounding exploitative conditions in sweatshops.

This plays out differently within the ranks of the industry's hierarchy. Management may try to appease their workers through parties and beauty contests, attempting to create an appearance of "friendship". Interestingly, many of these are held on Labour Day, when workers are traditionally likely to demonstrate and demand better wages and work conditions.

Open resistance has led to better minimum wages and improved monitoring systems to ensure compliance with labour laws, but it has not been without casualties. In 2014, five demonstrators died when police opened fire indiscriminately on a crowd of demonstrators. And even as the garment sector is increasingly formalised, scrutinised and monitored, an underbelly of the industry has sprouted. Unscrupulous business owners work to circumvent laws and regulations and cut costs through the use of sub-contractors, who have set up unregistered, nameless, and literally windowless factories (Kashyap, 2016).

Individual forms of resistance have also been utilised. Withdrawal is one. Women demonstrate high mobility between factories. The longer they have lived and worked in the city, their growing social networks allow women to access new and perhaps better jobs when they become dissatisfied with their current work conditions. Insults, shaming and personal offense due to a bad relationship with a line leader, are all valid reasons to move on. There is also marked mobility into new industries. The director of a local organisation that had interviewed women employed in the sex industry, shared that it was discovered that 70 percent of them initially migrated to the city to work in the garment industry. Higher earnings and better working conditions were the reasons given for their change of occupation.

STRADDLING URBAN LIVING AND RURAL VALUES

As Cambodia straddles the threshold between poverty and development, her people are confronted by the challenges that modernisation and urbanisation bring. While migration is blurring the clear lines between rural and urban spaces, thereby threatening traditional social norms, it is also providing new opportunities.

Much of the relevant literature emphasises the negative outcomes of women in migration. There are many possible motivations for migration, and it may be unclear who in the family makes the final decision. But the inequalities, exploitation and abuse sit alongside the increase of women's participation in the economic sphere and their economic empowerment, and positive changes in gender norms. Watching women transported in cattle trucks is appalling, but remittances allow families to build latrines, send children to school and perhaps buy a television. Gifts of kitchenware are proudly displayed in homes, women come home with confidence, and are consulted in decision-making in the household and community.

Despite economic and traditional social constraints, Cambodian women are socially and geographically mobile: moving flexibly between village and city, between factories and sectors. Social mobility is being achieved and identities are morphing to give meaning to changed women's lives.

Women as agents continually ascribe new meaning to tradition and culture, weaving in their ideals and dreams for independence, freedom and participation. They have balanced capital ambitions, participated in new forms of consumption, yet continue to find cultural acceptance. A young woman who is strong and assertive in the city may dress down when returning to her village, keep a lower tone of voice, and behave more demurely. This is all to preserve her marketability as a marriage-worthy, untainted village girl.

The garment factory floor is a site for individual oppression, but also individual responsibility. Here is a mass of women who can, if they dare, hold the future of Cambodia in their hands. It is the conclusion of this essay that migration to work in the garment factories has led much to the empowerment of Cambodian women.

Guiding Mission Alliance's Trajectory of Work

A critical question is the degree of agency a woman has in determining her own future. Systems, economies and worlds often seek to subject women, restricting their choices and opportunities. We must do all we can to help women realise their agency. We need to walk alongside them in the choices they make. If a woman chooses to migrate, let us help her make an informed choice, and migrate safely. If she needs a job, let us work to extend the choices available to her, by enabling her to get better access to quality education, vocational training, and credit. If she becomes trapped in oppressive and exploitative employment, we must help her to become aware of her rights and develop the confidence to speak up. It is also crucial that in our calling as development practitioners we do not reduce the people we seek to serve to mere objects, passive recipients of our well-meaning, good intentioned work. We must remember at all times that the women we serve have the right to be all that God intends for them to be. Free will and agency is foundational to that right.

REFERENCES

ADB. 2014. *Cambodia Country Poverty Analysis 2014.* Retrieved October 24, 2017. (https://www.adb.org/sites/default/files/institutional-document/151706/cambodia-country-poverty-analysis-2014.pdf)

---. 2017. *Cambodia Needs More Support to Achieve its Gender Equality Goals.* Retrieved November 3, 2017. (https://www.adb.org/news/cambodia-needs-more-support-achieve-its-gender-equality-goals)

Addati, L, Florence Bonnet, Ekkehard Ernst, Rossana Merola and Pei Man Jessica Wan. 2016. *Women at Work: Trends 2016.* Geneva: International Labour Office.

Cambodia Rural Urban Migration Project 2011. Phnom Penh: Ministry of Planning Cambodia.

Chandler, D. 1978. "Songs at the Edge of the Forest: Perceptions of Order in Three Cambodian Texts." Pp. 31–46 in *At the Edge of the Forest: Essays on Cambodia, History, and Narrative in Honor of David Chandler,* edited by Anne Ruth Hansen and Judy Ledgerwood. Ithaca, NY: Cornell University Press.

Chey, E. n.d. *Cambodia: The Status of Khmer Women.* Retrieved November 3, 2017. (http://www.mekong.net/cambodia/women.htm)

Derks, A. 2008. *Khmer Women on the Move.* Honolulu, HI: University of Hawai'i Press.

Ebihara, M. &. Judy Ledgerwood. 2002. "Aftermaths of Genocide: Cambodian Villagers." Pp. 272–291 in *Annihilating Difference: The Anthropology of Genocide,* edited by Alexander Hinton. Berkeley, CA: University of California Press.

Final Report Cambodia Socio-Economic Survey 2015. 2016. Retrieved October 2, 2017. (https://www.nis.gov.kh/nis/CSES/Final%20Report%20CSES%202015.pdf)

General Population Census of Cambodia 2008. Phnom Penh: Kingdom of Cambodia.

Gorman, S. with Pon D. & Sok K. 1999. *Gender and Development in Cambodia: An Overview.* Phnom Penh: Cambodia Development Resource Institute.

Grez, E. E. n.d. *Gender, Migration & Work.* Retrieved November 5, 2017. (http://www.yorku.ca/ishd/Introduction.Migration.work.pdf)

Hai, K. E. 2017. *Cambodia: Demographic Dividend and Aging Population.* Retrieved October 26, 2017. (https://cambodiancorner.wordpress.com/2017/01/11/demographicdividend/)

Hang, L. 2012. *Measuring Women Status and Gender Statistics in Cambodia.* Presented at the Global Forum on Gender Statistics, Dead Sea, Jordan. Cambodia: National Institute of Statistics, Ministry of Planning.

International Labour Organization. 2006. *Women and Work in the Garment Factory.* Phnom Penh: ILO.

---. 2007. *Policy Brief on Youth Employment in Cambodia.* Phnom Penh: ILO.

In Focus: Women & Poverty, UN Women. n.d. Retrieved November 3, 2017. (http://beijing20.unwomen.org/en/in-focus/poverty)

Kashyap, A. 2016. *The Secret Underbelly of the Cambodian Garment Industry.* Retrieved November 3, 2017. (https://www.hrw.org/news/2016/10/24/secret-underbelly-cambodian-garment-industry)

Drs. Lawreniuk S & Laurie Parsons. 2016. *I Know I Cannot Quit: The Prevalence and Productivity Cost of Sexual Harassment to the Cambodian Garment Industry.* Canberra: Care International. Retrieved November 3, 2017. (https://www.care.org.au/wp-content/uploads/2017/04/SHCS_Brief-Women-Cambodia-Garment-Industry-March-2017_CA.pdf)

Ledgerwood, J. 1994. "Gender Symbolism and Culture Change: Viewing the Virtuous Woman in the

Khmer Story 'Mea Yoeng.'" Pp. 119–128 in *Cambodian Culture Since 1975: Homeland and Exile*, edited by C. A. May Ebihara. Ithaca, NY: Cornell University Press.

Ledgerwood, J. n.d. *Understanding Cambodia: Social Hierarchy, Patron-Client Relationships and Power*. Retrieved October 26, 2017. (http://www.seasite.niu.edu/khmer/Ledgerwood/patrons.htm)

---. n.d. *Women in Cambodian Society*. Retrieved October 21, 2017. (http://www.seasite.niu.edu/khmer/ledgerwood/women.htm)

Ledgerwood, J & Vijghen, J. 1990. *Changing Khmer Conceptions of Gender: Women, Stories and the Moral Order*. Anthropology Department, Cornell University.

Manet, S. C. 2017. *Garment Sectors Lackluster Results*. Retrieved November 3, 2017. (http://www.khmertimeskh.com/5074380/garment-sectors-lackluster-results/)

Mills, M. B. 1999. *Thai Women in the Global Labour Force: Consuming Desires, Contested Identities*. New Brunswick: Rutgers University Press.

National Institute of Statistics. 2014. *2014 Cambodia Demographic and Health Survey*. Retrieved November 3, 2017. (https://www.dhsprogram.com/pubs/pdf/SR226/SR226.pdf)

National Institute of Statistics. 2016. *Cambodia Socio-Economic Survey 2015*. Phnom Penh: Ministry of Planning.

Ollman, B. 1999. *Market Economy: Advantages and Disadvantages*. Retrieved November 2, 2017. (https://www.nyu.edu/projects/ollman/docs/china_speech2.php)

Sassen, S. 1984. "Notes on the Incorporation of Third World Women into Wage Labour through Immigration and Offshore Production." Pp. 111–131 in *Globalization and its Discontents*. New York, NY: The New Press.

SHCS Brief: Women in Cambodia's Garment Industry. 2016. Retrieved November 3, 2017. (https://www.care.org.au/wp-content/uploads/2017/04/SHCS_Brief-Women-Cambodia-Garment-Industry-March-2017_CA.pdf)

They, Kheam & Emily Treleaven. 2013. *A CRUMP Report: Women and Migration in Cambodia*. Phnom Penh: Ministry of Planning.

UNDP. 2016. *Human Development Reports*. Retrieved October 25, 2017. (http://www.hdr.undp.org/en/indicators/68606)

UNIFEM, World Bank, ADB, UNDP, DFID. 2004. *A Fair Share for Women: Cambodia Gender Assessment*. Retrieved 10 23, 2017. (https://www.adb.org/documents/fair-share-women-cambodia-gender-assessment)

Vachon, M. 2017. *Baby Boom after Khmer Rouge Led to Cambodia's Young Population*. Retrieved October 26, 2017. (https://www.cambodiadaily.com/news/baby-boom-after-khmer-rouge-led-to-cambodias-young-population-127415/)

Walque, D. d. 2004. *The Long-term Legacy of the Khmer Rouge Period in Cambodia*. Phnom Penh: The World Bank, Development Research Group.

World Bank. 2017, Retrieved 10 13, 2017. (http://www.worldbank.org/en/country/cambodia/overview)

---. n.d. *Country Profile: World Development Indicators*. Retrieved 10 13, 2017, (http://databank.worldbank.org/data/Views/Reports/ReportWidgetCustom.aspx?Report_Name=CountryProfile&Id=b450fd57&tbar=y&dd=y&inf=n&zm=n&country=KHM)

World Bank: Age Dependency Ratio. 2016. Retrieved October 26, 2017. (https://data.worldbank.org/indicator/SP.POP.DPND?locations=KH)

Zimmer, Z, John Knodel, Kiry Sovan Kim, Sina Puch. 2005. *The Impact of Past Conflicts and Social*

Disruption in Cambodia on the Current Generation of Older Adults. Ann Arbour, MI: Institute for Social Research, University of Michigan.

Zimmer, Z. 2012. *Migration in Cambodia: Report of the Cambodian Rural Urban Project.* Phnom Penh: Ministry of Planning.

Church, Politics, Justice & Mission in Nepal

Peter Lockwood

Introduction

" The LORD said to Joshua the son of Nun, Moses' assistant, "Moses my servant is dead. Now therefore arise, go over this Jordan, you and all these people, into the land that I am giving to them, to the people of Israel.'" (Josh. 1:1b–2, ESV). Joshua stood at a crossroads. It had been a long and gruelling journey to this point, but a new future stretched ahead, no doubt filling him with both trepidation and a galvanising sense of opportunity. In a similar way, the country of Nepal currently finds itself at such a crossroads.

Political Context and Constitution (2015)

The past 20 years has been a period of significant political instability and turmoil in Nepal. Nepal's Maoist Communist Party launched a ten-year civil war (1996–2006) to replace the Royal Parliamentary System with a People's Socialist Republic. This devastating conflict resulted in over

12,000 deaths, the displacement of more than 100,000 people, and the destruction of important public infrastructures. On February 1, 2002, King Gyanendra—who acceded to the throne following the murder of his brother King Birendra and other members of the royal family on June 1, 2001—suspended Parliament, appointed a government led by himself, and enforced martial law. In April 2006, a countrywide uprising called the *Loktantra Andolan* sparked massive demonstrations against King Gyanendra's autocratic rule (Sengupta, 2006). On April 21, 2006, King Gyanendra declared that, "power would be returned to the people" and announced the reinstatement of the House of Representatives. On May 19, 2006, the Parliament assumed total legislative power and gave executive power to the Government of Nepal. For centuries Nepal had been a Hindu Kingdom, but this was abrogated, and Nepal was declared a secular state. Prime Minister G.P. Koirala issued a letter on July 19, 2006, to the United Nations announcing the Nepalese Government's intentions to hold elections to form a Constituent Assembly and to draft and promulgate a new constitution.

The first Constitutional Assembly was established in 2008, and there were high hopes amongst the people for a new Nepal. However, it was dissolved in 2012, having failed to agree on a new constitution. Dr Adhikari, Dean of Kathmandu University School of Law stated that, "the country has been held hostage by the political parties and the political leaders, who have put their and their parties', and later in the constitution-making process, their ethnic and divisive interests first, when they should have put the country's national interests central in all their dealings and decisions" (Bipin Adhikari, 2012).

Following fresh elections, the second Constitutional Assembly commenced its term in November 2013. Despite political fragility, frequent strikes, and the 2015 Gorkha earthquake,[1] the new constitution was finally promulgated on September 20, 2015. Minority ethnic groups,

---

1   There were two major earthquakes, M7.8 on April 25 and M7.3 on May 12, 2015, causing the death of about 9,000 people, injuring over 22,000, and resulting in loss and damage including approximately 880,000 partially or fully damaged houses equivalent to USD 7 billion.

including the Terai-based Madheshi people[2] objected strongly, claiming that the Constitution discriminated against them, particularly regarding citizenship provisions and the proposed boundaries of provinces. Violence broke out in several regional towns, and a prolonged blockade of the Indian border caused immense damage to the national economy and much hardship for ordinary people. In 2017, after much political wrangling and "arm twisting", there was finally an agreement on the political boundaries for the new local-level and provincial-level governments. It paved the way for the local elections, which were held on May 14, June 28 and September 18, 2017. These were the first local-level elections since the 2015 Constitution, and the first recognised local-level elections since 2002. Following successful local, provincial, and national elections in 2017, K.P. Oli of the Unified Marxist-Leninist Party was sworn in as Prime Minister on February 25, 2018. On that day he became the 27th Prime Minister in the past 28 years. Oli combined his party with the Communist Party of Nepal–Maoist to form a majority Government. This Government has proven remarkably stable and is anticipated to remain intact for the full five-year term of the Parliament. In August 2018, the Government replaced the out-dated national legal code, *"Muluki Ain"*, with the new Criminal Code. They are in the process of passing implementation laws, but there continues to be considerable debate, delay, and concern at the regressive nature of some provisions. The criminalisation of routine news reporting, citizenship discrimination based on gender, a ban on religious conversion, and a weakening of the judiciary are continuing areas of debate. The local- and provincial-level governments are new, and they continue to formulate their legislation and demand their budget allocations under the new Constitution. In the midst of these demanding changes, there is unprecedented scope for local-level communities and churches to influence the writing of legislation, as well as the allocation and use of local-level budgets.

---

2   The Madheshis are a generic people group of Indian ancestry that live on the border area between India and Nepal. They have experienced centuries of marginalisation and discrimination, and have responded with phases of political agitation for dignity and equal rights.

The Constitution of Nepal 2015 is the country's seventh. It is a lengthy document with 308 Articles, 9 Annexes, and a Preamble. But, as Adhikari reflects, "it builds [on] the past and has many new and progressive provisions" (Binod Adhikari, 2017:2). The Preamble of the 2015 Constitution states that its primary objective is, "to ensure economic equality, prosperity and social justice, by eliminating discrimination based on class, caste, region, language, religion and gender and all forms of caste-based untouchability" (Ministry of Law, Justice and Parliamentary Affairs, 2015: Preamble). The Constitution has adopted "rights-based" language, and there are several vital, fundamental rights that have been strengthened, improved, or added. Article 18 commits to the general right of equality and non-discrimination, with specific mention of several disadvantaged ethnic groups (Dalits, Adibasi, Janjatis, Madheshi, Tharus, Muslims), and a general reference to children, gender and disabled people. Article 38 secures the rights of women, and covers equal lineage, safe motherhood and reproductive health, freedom from any physical, mental, sexual or psychological violence, and the right to participate in State structures and Bodies (ibid., Article 38(1–4)). There is also a comprehensive right to education, health, employment and social security (ibid., Article 38(5)). Significantly, it is the first time both spouses have equal rights to property and in family affairs (ibid., Article 38(6)). It also explicitly prohibits child marriage and instates a legal age for marriage (ibid., Article 39(5)), both of which are progressive provisions. These are some of the new Human Rights provisions, but the Constitution also addresses important areas such as the Rights of Dalits, the Right of Language, and the Culture and Right of Citizenship.

Despite the many inclusive and progressive provisions under the new Constitution, there remain some areas of concern, which have been highlighted in an open letter to the Government of Nepal from Amnesty International (Griffiths, 2015). The Constitution states that every person has, "the right to profess, practice, and protect his or her religion" (Ministry of Law, Justice and Parliamentary Affairs, 2015: Article 1). Of specific concern for the Church is that it goes on to stipulate that when practising their chosen religion, individuals cannot engage in any practice which is, "contrary to public health, decency, and morality" or "disturb the public law and order situation" (Ministry of Law, Justice and Parliamentary Affairs, 2015: Article 26(3)). The clause is extremely broad and makes it a criminal offence punishable by fines, imprisonment, and expulsion in the case of foreign nationals, to convert a person of one religion to another religion or to disturb the religion of other people. In the history of Nepal's constitutions and law, proselytisation has continued to be illegal. The new Criminal Code came into effect from July 2017 and has even stronger anti-conversion provision, with the criminalisation of unintentionally converting people, and vague anti-blasphemy provisions involving the hurting of religious feelings. The anti-proselytising and anti-conversion legal constraints, which have been evident in the previous Constitutions, have been clearly reaffirmed and upheld. It is within this climate of increased pressure and uncertainty that the Church in Nepal continues to worship and witness.

The Church in Nepal

There has been remarkable growth in the Nepali Church over the past 70 years. The 1951 census listed zero Christians, and this increased to 458 in 1961. By 2001, there were nearly 102,000, and by the last census in 2011 this further increased to 375,000. Today there is a wide range of estimates as to the number of Christians in Nepal, and some believe that there are over 2,000,000 practising believers (R. Rai, 2016). Operation World gives the total number of Christians in Nepal at just over 850,000 ("Nepal", 2017) with an annual growth rate of 5.3 percent, which would confirm it, "as the fastest-growing religion in Nepal, and one of the fastest-growing churches both in South Asia and globally" (ibid.).

Dr Rongong, one of the early Nepali Church leaders, reflects on the embryonic start of the church in Nepal, and its early years of growth through severe persecution, saying, "Churches in Nepal began as indigenous churches. They were independent in that they had no official connection to established churches or denominations outside the country. The structure of the church worship was contextualised as far as possible" (Rongong et al., 2012:75).

When Nepal opened its doors to the international community in the early 1950s, two of the founding missions, International Nepal Fellowship and United Mission to Nepal were invited by the Government to engage in medical and education work. They simultaneously made it clear that evangelism, proselytisation and preaching were unwelcome. According to Rongong, the early Nepali Church leaders and pioneer missionaries decided that the Church in Nepal should be indigenous. It was to remain separate from mission organisations and missionaries should provide a supporting role and not be in leadership. Consequently, the mission organisations focused on establishing hospitals, schools and rural development works, while the local Church focused on evangelism and church planting. The two worked well together and there has developed over the years considerable trust, support and mutual cooperation.

During its relatively short history, the growth of the Church in Nepal has occurred in the context of the severe legal prohibitions described above, which make it a criminal offence to change one's religion and to encourage others to convert to a new religion. In 1963, Nepal codified all its civil, criminal, religious and customary laws in what is called the *Muluki Ain*. As the country moved from being a closed feudal society, this Code introduced several human-right provisions that abolished many types of discrimination including the caste system, and recognised the customary rules and practices of specific indigenous communities.

Under the *Muluki Ain*, if someone attempted to convert another individual to their religion, they could be punished with three years' imprisonment. And if they successfully converted someone to another religion, they could face six years' imprisonment. It also stated that foreign nationals who attempted to convert a Nepalese citizen to another religion would be expelled from Nepal after serving a six-year prison sentence (Thapa, 2010). Although the Nepali church was birthed and grew under these weighty legal restraints, it has always placed a priority on evangelism

(Rongong et al., 2012:76). The spread of the gospel in Nepal is primarily due to the passion of the local Church and the passion of its members. Significantly, "the prohibition of conversion and the reality of persecution from the outset prevented nominalism" (Barclay, 2009:193), and the cost of genuine faith in Christ promoted urgency, and the prioritisation of evangelism.

Coupled with these legal restraints, there continues to be negative media coverage towards the Church in Nepal. An accusation regularly levelled by the Nepali media is that conversion to Christianity is influenced by a desire for material gain. Recent examples of this can be read in two articles published in the Nepali Times newspaper by Brot Coburn, "Preaching on high" and Om Rai, "The golden age of the gospel" (Coburn, 2017; O. A. Rai, 2017). The international media have also published similar arguments. An article in *The Guardian* quotes a Nepali Hindu priest who accuses Christians of "using money to promote Christianity" (Pattisson, 2017).

In actual fact, most Nepali men and women who convert to Christianity, suffer loss in material terms. They are often disinherited from their families, ostracised from their communities, and discriminated against in employment (Kehrberg, 2000:105–109; Perry, 2000:103; Rongong et al., 2012, Chapter 8). The Nepali Church is experiencing the cost of discipleship that Jesus talked about in Luke 14:25–33. Persecution, discrimination, and isolation are some of the real costs that Christians have suffered, and continue to experience in Nepal.

Integral Mission

It is recognised that the Nepali Church is exemplary in its evangelical zeal, but some of its inevitable weaknesses have also been identified. It has been recognised that local churches will often remain insular and largely isolated from their local communities (Barclay, 2009:192). Church members, because of the persecution they face, often hold hostile beliefs about their former religions, and experience hostility from those communities (J.

Rai, 2017). Advocates of integral mission are urging Nepali churches to rid themselves of this unfortunate dichotomy, and to address what John Stott described as the "unnecessary polarisation between our Christian evangelistic and social responsibilities" (Stott, 2014:57). Jean-Paul Heldt has suggested that

> ...there is no longer a need to qualify mission as "holistic", nor to distinguish between "mission" and "holistic mission". Mission is "holistic", and therefore "holistic mission", is de facto mission. Proclamation alone, apart from any social concern, may be perceived as a distortion, a truncated version of the true gospel, a parody and travesty of good news, lacking relevance for the real problems of real people living in the real world. On the other end of the spectrum, exclusive focus on transformation and advocacy may result in social and humanitarian activism, void of any spiritual dimension. Both approaches are unbiblical; they deny the wholeness of human nature of human beings created in the image of God. Since we are created "whole", and since the Fall affects our total humanity in all its dimensions, then redemption, restoration, and mission can, by definition, only be holistic (2004:166).

Micah Global offers a succinct definition of integral mission,

> Integral mission or holistic transformation is the proclamation and demonstration of the gospel. It is not simply that evangelism and social involvement are to be done alongside each other. Rather, in integral mission our proclamation has social consequences as we call people to love and repentance in all areas of life. And our social involvement has evangelistic consequences as we bear witness to the transforming grace of Jesus Christ. (Micah Network Declaration, 2001)

Both Heldt and Micah Global have articulated the importance of integrating the two biblical teachings of evangelism and social involvement, arguing convincingly that one cannot properly exist without the other. Heldt argues that prefixing "holistic" to "mission" is not a necessity, as mission is or should be by its very nature, *holistic*. However, the use of the term *integral mission* could have great value in challenging the Nepali Church to understand and explore the breadth and depth of meaning within the concept of the "mission of God".

ADVOCACY, BIBLICAL JUSTICE, AND THE CHURCH

In reference to contextual and liberation theologies, Christopher Wright observes that,

> What many of these newer theologies have in common is their advocacy stance. That is, they arise from the conviction that it is fundamental to biblical faith to take a stand alongside the victims of injustice in any form. Thus, the Bible is to be read with a liberationist hermeneutic—that is, with a concern to liberate people from oppression and exploitation (2006:42).

Andrew Sloane examines the theological arguments used to oppose Christian involvement in advocating for justice. On the right of the theological spectrum, the argument is made that the sole mission of the Church is the "verbal proclamation of the gospel—and that justice and advocacy are other people's business" (Sloane, 2011:1). Others on the theological left stress "the illegitimacy of Christians using power in God's name" and the need for "incarnational identification with the poor in their weakness and vulnerability" (ibid.:2). Wright argues that both extremes are thin and fragmentary, and fail to consider the wealth of scriptural evidence expressing God's concern for the poor, and the responsibility of the Church to act on behalf of the voiceless, the poor, and the marginalised (ibid.:2).

"The concern for justice pervades the entire Old Testament (For example, Exod. 22:2–3; Deut. 24:17–19; Lev. 19:15, 30–34)" (Wright, 2004). The words, "justice" (*misphat*) and, "righteousness" (*tsedaqah*) are paired together in the Old Testament and in their various noun and adjective forms are used over 400 times (Harris, Jr. and Waltke, 1980: 1870–1879, 2443–2445). The combination of these two words, "*misphat*" and, "*tsedaqah*" form a single but complex and comprehensive biblical idea. It is variably translated into English as, "social justice", "primary justice", "biblical justice" or simply, "justice". In the Old Testament, the idea of social justice was never an abstract concept but a dynamic for living. It was an exhortation to live justly, and work for the practical outworking of justice for all.

The Old Testament portrays "YHWH" as a God of justice and righteousness, characteristics that are perfectly reflected in the work and person of Jesus Christ. In declaring himself as the Messiah (Matt. 12:17–21), Christ was tasked with proclaiming good news to the poor, bringing release to the vulnerable (blind) (Luke 4:17–21), and inaugurating the Kingdom of God, which is invariably characterised as a Kingdom of justice and righteousness. Gushee and Stassen (2016:131–146) have advocated that Jesus taught and demonstrated at least four strands of justice. The mission of Jesus was firstly non-violent, yet he confronted those in authority who orchestrated and condoned violence (Matthew 23:31ff; Luke 23:31ff). Secondly, he challenged the wealthy, and highlighted how they had oppressed the poor in the acquisition of money. He criticised their over-reliance on wealth, and said it ultimately demonstrated their rejection of God (Mark 12: 38–40; Mark 10:25; Luke 16:14ff). Thirdly, Jesus condemned those who abused power by dominating others. The fourth strand is seen in the example that Jesus set by the people he included, as he not only healed the ostracised, but accepted them into his community.

UMN's Embraces Church Community Mobilisation (CCM) Programme

The primary purpose of Tearfund UK's Church Community Mobilisation (CCM) is to envision and equip local churches to alleviate poverty, fight against injustice, and transform their communities. Since 2010, United Mission to Nepal has been adopting and adapting the CCM process as a resource to achieve its aim of moving the missiology and mission practice of Nepali Churches in the direction of integral mission.

From 2010 to 2012, UMN's Integral Mission Team began to learn about, formulate and design a culturally appropriate CCM programme that would provide orientation for churches and faith-based partner organisations. During the early stage, there was a general familiarisation of the Church Community Mobilisation process and the manuals with the Integral Mission team. This was followed by a pilot programme, which ran from July 2012 to July 2015. UMN worked with local partner organisations and churches in six districts of Nepal: Bajhang, Dhading, Doti, Rukum, Rupendehi and Sunsari. At the end of this pilot period, there was a substantial review and re-focusing of the process, which resulted in the Sangsangai Programme (or the "all together" programme). It commenced in July 2015 and continued for three years working with two partners, the Dhading Christian Society (DCS), Isai Samaj Nawalparasi (ISN), as well as 23 churches in Dhading and Nawalparasi districts.

In the wake of its proven effectiveness, United Mission to Nepal has introduced CCM to churches in Nepal and translated its training materials into Nepali. CCM has evolved into *Sangsangai*, with the aim of capacity building Nepali pastors, church leaders and members of church congregations to work with and within their local communities, inspiring them to be creative agents of social and spiritual transformation. The vision is that both church and community will benefit from an increase in mutual cooperation and involvement together.

It is envisaged that the Church will increase in confidence, as it develops deepening relationships and team-building skills within its members and with people in the community. With this joint cooperation, the local churches can become more effective in identifying resources to meet the needs of its local community. By strengthening the skills, knowledge, and confidence of the church pastor, the leadership and membership, this process is designed to inspire and promote a broader vision of God's work throughout the Church. As the church grows, matures, and becomes increasingly active in helping and doing good to others, it will build bridges of trust and understanding that should ultimately have a positive influence within Nepali communities. It is hoped that all members of the Nepali community will experience a growing sense of hope, well-being, self-esteem and self-reliance.

The next section provides a brief overview of Tearfund UK's Church Community Mobilisation programme and then an examination of UMN's application of CCM in the Nepal context.

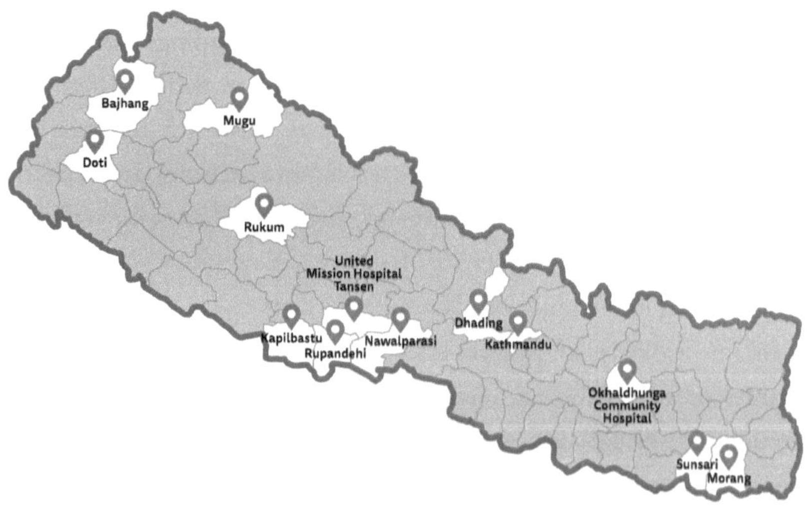

Figure 1. Map of Nepal, showing UMN's Working Areas

Outline and Overview of the Sangsangai Programme

Thus far the programme has been successfully implemented in over 35 countries and, as recently as 2014, has carried out an extensive evidence-based study of the impact of the Church Community Mobilisation process in Tanzania. This report concluded that "the process has then gone on to help people realise tangible benefits across several domains of change within a comprehensive poverty and well-being framework" (Scott, Foley, Brooks, & Batchelor, 2014:20).

The CCM process has five distinct phases. The first stage is the "envisioning and equipping" of the church. The key to this first phase is the development of a clear biblical understanding of the nature and mission of the church, which then results in the church becoming impassioned to address the needs of the poor and promote God's justice in an unjust world corrupted by sin. This programme seeks to address a missing emphasis in the overall work of the Nepali Church by promoting the concept and biblical basis of "Integral Mission".

The second stage, "envisioning the community", aims to assist communities on a journey to assess both their needs and resources. While there are suggested Bible studies and activities, there should be sensitivity regarding their use based on the local context. These first two stages lead into the third stage, "dreaming dreams", and planning for action. The church and community work together to establish a future vision and outline plans on how to achieve it.

The fourth stage is all about "taking action" and ensuring that plans are properly designed and that there is proper implementation leading to the expected positive changes.

Finally, the fifth stage, "evaluation", assesses the whole process and its impact, focusing on how the church and community worked together. It also highlights ways to improve planning and the execution of projects that improve the lives of the whole community. This stage is expected to serve as a springboard for a deepening relationship between church and community, one that equips them to further the alleviation of poverty, and ensure the marginalised are heard and their rights are upheld.

One of the critical activities that is repeated in each of the first four stages is "learning and reflection". The process is not about outsiders coming in and promoting a programme or solution. Rather, it invites the church to take the lead and involves the collaborative participation of both the church and local community. As the process is relational, this activity is vital for sharing quantitative and qualitative information with the senior church leadership, the members and the community. By introducing this period of reflection at each stage it encourages transparency, openness and honesty. It promotes the importance of generating ideas and conducting a review on what has worked well and what needs improving. The long-term sustainability of the process is reliant on the "learning and reflection" activities as the church and community continue to generate needs, gather resources and implement appropriate actions and plans.

UMN's Application of the Sangsangai Approach

During this initial period, UMN provided no financial support to either the local partner organisations or the local churches but facilitated awareness-raising and training on the Coordinator's and Facilitator's Guides. For most of the churches and faith-based partner organisations, integral mission was a very new concept. Sadly, there was a perception that as UMN were promoting this programme, it should also provide funding and resources.

This pilot programme introduced the local churches and UMN's faith-based partners to the idea that mission was more than evangelism but included reaching out to the local community and working alongside the community to identify and address the needs of everyone. The impact of this orientation with the different churches was mixed and varied geographically. Rural churches were more receptive than urban-centred churches to the *Sangsangai* process, probably because they tended to have a much stronger sense of community. Town and city churches were slower to engage in the process, preferring to focus on their church planting work and the needs of their church members (Khanal, 2017; D. Rai, 2017; J. Rai, 2017).

Some churches moved ahead of the defined *Sangsangai* process and jumped straight to implementing quick fix community-based development projects, for example community drinking water schemes. Undoubtedly, these projects addressed real community needs. However, a fundamental element of the *Sangsangai* process was encouraging churches to think through the theology and implications of the church's evangelistic and social responsibilities. There was a significant underlying tension and expectation from the local churches and partners that United Mission to Nepal should be providing additional financial resources for community development projects for their faith-based partner organisations and associated churches.

In 2014 Tearfund, UK, conducted an external evaluation of the pilot programme that resulted in 11 recommendations to consider during the design of the follow-up programme. Underlying these recommendations was the increasing perception from UMN's staff, local pastors and partner organisation staff of the importance of *Sangsangai* as a critical component of United Mission to Nepal's integral mission work. The evaluation recommended that local churches needed to develop a clear desire and ownership of the process with a more specific strategy on implementation and more formalised support of the church-based facilitators.

In the *Sangsangai* process, the facilitators are the key people in terms of successfully operationalising the programme, so it was crucial to develop and implement clear criteria for their selection. In Nepal, there is a phrase, *aphno manche*, which means someone that is your own person, relative, caste, kin or family member. This phrase sums up an important working principle of Nepali culture, where preference, patronage and benefits are given, and loyalty and obedience are expected. The church is susceptible to this cultural norm, and it was observed during the pilot *Sangsangai* programme that in some churches the pastor's family members were favoured for selection. Additionally, it was recognised that a selected facilitator must be a respected and influential member of the local church. Otherwise there is a risk that the members of the congregation would continuously be looking to the pastor for approval of the process and decisions.

The evaluation addresses another essential aspect of the *Sangsangai* process—the selection of churches and supporting partner organisations. Churches must demonstrate that they see the need to undertake this journey and that they "own" the process and understand that the resources for implementing community development work are generated by the church.

The final key recommendation was that churches and communities, when developing and implementing programmes, should start small and carefully monitor and evaluate the whole process. Only when there is a good understanding by all parties of the process should groups attempt to implement larger-scale projects.

The external evaluation in 2014 was necessary, not only for developing the follow-up *Sangsangai* programme but also for feeding into the development of UMN's 2015–2020 Strategic Plan. The Government of Nepal first invited UMN to work in Nepal in 1954. Since then there has been a government requirement that all International Non-Government Organisations must renew their Five-Year General Agreement with the Government every five years, and this must include a detailed Five-Year Strategic Plan.

UMN's current strategic plan (2015–2020) develops four key result areas for its integral mission work (United Mission to Nepal Strategy 2015–2020, 2015: sec. 3.3.6):

- The concept and practice of integral mission integrated into the curricula of Nepali theological organisations;

- The capacity of faith-based networks and organisations to serve Poorest People Living with Poverty (PPLP) strengthened;

- Churches and communities working together to address the needs of Poorest People Living with Poverty (PPLP) using local resources;

- Young people equipped with relevant knowledge, attitudes and leadership skills to address the needs of the PPLP.

The follow-up on the *Sangsangai* programme started in July 2015, ran for three years, worked with two partners—Dhading Christian Society (DCS) and Isai Samaj Nawalparasi (ISN)—and involved a total of 23 churches in Dhading and Nawalparasi districts. One of the many improvements in promoting the *Sangsangai* process has been the development of its Operating Principles. Based on these principles, a church and its related partner sign a Memorandum of Understanding, which includes clear definitions of roles and responsibilities between both parties. UMN's Integral Mission Team, with input from DCS and ISN, developed a detailed training plan with workbooks and manuals. While there are ten operating principles, there are three underlying key ideas. Firstly, the *Sangsangai* process is a journey reflecting on God's Word to discover and hear what God is saying to the local church regarding how they use God's provision in their local communities. Secondly, the process is based on an action and reflection learning cycle, with stress on the importance of listening to everyone's voice. Thirdly, the focus is on engaging the whole community with concern for the poor and marginalised promoting inclusion for all.

The programme is reviewed on an annual basis. The second-year annual donor report (Khanal, Karki and Singh, 2017) has highlighted many achievements and case stories where the church has worked with and assisted the local community in social action. There are some cases where financial support from the church had been given to assist people in medical treatment, roofing material for houses and educational materials for children of poor single-parent families. Four churches have been involved in the construction of local access roads. These roads have improved the ability of the local communities to transport vegetables and fruit to local markets and allowed more accessible transportation of building materials for construction and improvements on local housing. Two congregations mobilised the whole of the local villages to plant over 85,000 tree saplings in the local community forest. A church in west Dhading established a weekly savings scheme and the money collected is being used as a revolving fund, where members can take a loan with the agreement of paying it back with nominal interest payments. Several churches have repaired local infrastructures, such as water tanks, drinking water pipes and a suspended foot-trail bridge. In the following example, the foot-trail improved access to schools, local markets and roads. As recognition of this initiative the local government provided some funding, which allowed the church to construct a new building. The final example is New Life Church, Harbale in Nawalparai, which has initiated a communal vegetable garden, where everyone in the village (35 households) shares in the work and the produce.

As the programme enters its final year, the local churches have been navigating the establishment of the new local government policies, structures and personnel change. The newly elected officials, which include some Nepali Christians, are passionate about the development of their villages and are seeking good collaboration with local NGOs. In some areas, the local church has been recognised and allocated funds for their development work, and are valuable members of the community (Khanal, Karki and Singh, 2019). Not only has there been improved relationships at local government level, but there also continues to be a change in attitude in the local church. This has resulted in churches embracing social issues as their mission priorities and serving people regardless of their religious inclinations. With Christians serving the sick in hospital, older people in the villages, and younger students in public schools, the local church has become a centre of community (Khanal, Karki, and Singh, 2018). Its increasing engagement in the *Sangsangai* process has led to an organic shift from prioritising evangelism to practicing social action. Stott, in discussing evangelism and social responsibility, succinctly reminds us, "we have good biblical warrant to replace a rather naïve *either-or* with a mature *both-and*" (2014:64–65). As the local Church engages with the *Sangsangai* process, there is a deepening understanding and a change in attitude.

The author's interviews with Dipak Rai and Jiwan Rai, UMN's Integral Mission Officers in Nawalparasi and Dhading, respectively, were very encouraging. They have witnessed first-hand the positive impact in the community of local churches embracing the vision of integral mission.

Some churches have promoted and practiced collective leadership, but, reflecting the patriarchal nature of Nepali society, most power in the local congregation remains with the senior male pastors. The change will take time, but some churches already included women in their leadership committees. The interviews with Dipak Rai and Jiwan Rai explored the relationship between the image of God and human rights, and it was clear that human rights did not form part of the curriculum. In one conversation, human rights were described as what the secular world teaches. The final strand of the conversation revolved around how churches engage in advocacy and how churches were engaging with the newly elected local level governments. There was a broad spectrum of response, with some churches having little to no engagement with local authorities, to some churches having their pastor or senior church leaders being elected to the local government.

UMN is involved in the development and promotion of an Integral Mission module in association with some of the Nepal Bible Colleges. Dean Santosh Basnet of the Nepal Baptist Bible College was a member of the steering committee that helped develop the syllabus for this module. The module, which was introduced three years ago, is being taught as part of the college's four-year Bachelor of Theology Degree course, which is accredited through Asian Theological Association. There are currently 44 students (25 male and 18 female) studying for this degree. The author discussed the contents and impact of the module with Andrew Saunders who is a member of the teaching faculty of the College. He reported that a recent graduate, who is now a pastor of a rural Baptist church, encouraged his congregation to be more active in their local community. The church has initiated a regular litter picking programme, and increasingly more members of the wider community are joining the programme and seeking to improve the overall waste management of the village area. The content of the module was described as "a bit dry and theoretical": while it covers the major themes of biblical justice, creation, the fall, mission of God and the mission of the Church, the module has no practical application and does not cover human rights or advocacy.

CONCLUSION

There has been a monumental shift in Nepal's political situation over the last 20 years. The dynastic constitutional monarchy, in which the ruling monarch was revered and worshipped as a living Hindu god, has been replaced with a democratic Federal Republic. Previously every arena of life, encompassing the political, legal, social, and cultural spheres, was steeped in the Hindu religion, but it now proudly identifies itself as a secular state. The promulgation of the 2015 Constitution has proved an important milestone in the history of Nepal. It contains many significant provisions as it seeks to align with international Human Rights doctrine. Amidst these advances, the anti-proselytising and anti-conversion provisions in the new Constitution are a continuation of similar provisions from the previous constitutions, and reaffirm the government's commitment to deliberate discrimination against the Christian Church in Nepal. The Church in Nepal was born and has rapidly grown under legal, social, and cultural persecution. With similarities to the New Testament Church, these persecutions have served to strengthen church members who accept their suffering as an unavoidable part of their discipleship to Jesus. The witness and zeal of the Nepali Church has resulted in its passion for evangelism. Conversely, this sustained persecution has led local churches to become insular, self-protectionist, and at times to display an unhealthy hostility towards its local communities.

It is encouraging to see an increasing awareness of the Church's need for a more practical theology, and to this end the *Sangsangai* approach was successfully adopted by UMN and promoted through local partners and churches. It has been a way of empowering churches to begin engaging collaboratively with their local communities and advocating for their needs. The pilot programme had a slow start, showing limited effectiveness. This was mainly due to a lack of ownership by the churches, who perceived it as a UMN driven and funded programme. There were other problems identified, such as lack of procedures for selecting churches and facilitators.

The second phase of the *Sangsangai* programme has addressed these issues, and the participating churches have responded positively to the Bible-orientated training. The fruit from this has been the setting up, funding, and running of community projects by the 23 churches, in partnership with their local communities. Evaluating the programme to date, it seems that the facilitators steer communities towards issues of economic need rather than to issues of justice and power. For many individuals in churches, "human rights" is still quite an unknown concept. There remains an understandable reticence within the Church to be actively involved in advocacy, due to the sustained threat of persecution and deliberate discrimination under which it has worshipped. There is no foreseeable change to this climate, with the new Criminal Code of July 2019 having even stronger anti-conversion provisions, and extending criminalisation to the vague and undefined area of unintentionally converting people.

The expansion of the *Sangsangai* process at local church level and within Bible colleges will be a progressive development towards embracing the biblical call to advocate for others' rights and the rights of the poor. As churches begin to develop the Rights discourse, they will need to have an important discussion in terms of identifying whose rights need defending. Currently much of the Christian, political mobilisation is energised by "Christian rights", surrounding the issues of burial, conversion, and having Christmas recognised as a national holiday. Given the on-going political and social distrust of Christianity in Nepal, and the antagonistic promotion of current Christian Rights advocacy, it is recommended that the Church focuses its advocacy on addressing the underlying causes of poverty and injustice, and put much of their energy into fighting for the rights of others.

The church in Nepal is rapidly growing, yet the *Sangsangai* programme is only working within 23 local congregations. It is estimated that there are over six thousand churches in Nepal and so UMN is currently working on a small scale. The promoting and teaching of Integral Mission as a core module in the Nepal Bible colleges is a strategic expansion, as it profoundly influences the next generation of Nepali pastors and church leaders. However, the further expansion of *Sangsangai* at local-level churches needs to be examined and developed.

Joshua stood at a crossroads after a long and arduous journey, but with much work still to be accomplished. Nepal and the Nepali Church are at a similar point. So much has already been achieved—praise God. Nevertheless, there is still a long way to go. The command to, "be bold and be strong" (Josh. 1:9, NIV 1984) rings out. This is a fresh opportunity as Nepal develops its legislation under the provisions of the new Constitution. The Church can extend its vision, pray for courage and leadership, work to tackle both the root causes and the symptoms of poverty in partnership with their local communities, and advocate for the rights of the poor and marginalised with whom they live.

Abbreviations

GoN: Government of Nepal
INGO: International Non-Government Organisation
UDHR: Universal Declaration of Human Rights
PPLP: Poorest People Living with Poverty
UMN: United Mission to Nepal

REFERENCES

Adhikari, Binod. 2017. *Salient Features of the Constitution of Nepal 2015 (2072)*. Retrieved June 11, 2017 (http://bipinadhikari.com.np/quick_comments_ind.php?id=76)

Adhikari, Bipin. 2012. *Nepal Constituent Assembly Impasse: Comments on a Failed Process*. Retrieved November 10, 2017 (http://bipinadhikari.com.np/Archives/Books/Nepal_CA_Impasse.php)

Barclay, J. 2009. "The Church in Nepal: Analysis of its Gestation and Growth." *International Bulletin of Missionary Research*. 33(4): 189–194.

Coburn, B. 2017. "Preaching on High." Retrieved November 3, 2017 (http://nepalitimes.com/article/nation/preaching-on-high,3904)

Griffiths, D. 2015. *Open Letter to the New Prime Minister of Nepal: Amend Regressive Aspects of the Constitution*. Retrieved March 19, 2020 (https://www.amnesty.org/download/Documents/ASA3128022015ENGLISH.pdf)

Harris, R. L., G. L. Archer, Jr., & Waltke, B. K. 1980. *Theological Wordbook of the Old Testament*. Chicago, IL: Moody Press.

Heldt, J.-P. 2004. "Revisiting the "Whole Gospel": Toward a Biblical Model of Holistic Mission in the 21st century." *Missiology*. 32(2): 149–172. (https://doi.org/10.1177/009182960403200203)

Kehrberg, N. 2000. *The Cross in the Land of the Khukuri*. Kathmandu, Nepal: Ekta Books Distributors.

Khanal, D. 2017. *UMN's Integral Mission Team Leader*. Personal Interview on October 20, 2017

Khanal, D., Karki, J., & Singh, B. 2017. *IMCT Annual Report 2016–17*. United Mission to Nepal.

---. 2018. *IMCT Annual Report 2017–18*. United Mission to Nepal.

---. 2019. *IMCT Semi-Annual Report 2018–19*. United Mission to Nepal.

Micah Network Declaration on Integral Mission. 2001. Retrieved March 19, 2020. (https://www.micahnetwork.org/sites/default/files/doc/page/mn_integral_mission_declaration_en.pdf)

Ministry of Law, Justice and Parliamentary Affairs, Government of Nepal. 2015. *The Constitution of Nepal*. Retrieved March 19, 2020. (https://www.wipo.int/edocs/lexdocs/laws/en/np/np029en.pdf)

"Nepal." 2017. Retrieved November 4, 2017. (http://www.operationworld.org/country/nepa/owtext.html)

Pattisson, Pete. 2017. "They Use Money to Promote Christianity: Nepal's Battle for Souls." Retrieved March 19, 2020. (https://www.theguardian.com/global-development/2017/aug/15/they-use-money-to-promote-christianity-nepal-battle-for-souls)

Perry, C. L. 2000. *A Biographical History of the Church in Nepal*. Wheaton Graduate School, Kathmandu.

Rai, D. 2017. *UMN's Integral Mission Officer, Nawalparasi*. Personal Interview on November 3, 2017

Rai, J. 2017. *UMN's Integral Mission Officer, Dhading*. Personal Interview on November 3, 2017

Rai, O. A. 2017. "The Golden Age of the Gospel." Retrieved November 3 2017. (http://nepalitimes.com/article/nation/golden-age-of-gospel-christianity,3903)

Rai, R. 2016. "History of Christians in Nepal." Retrieved November 3, 2017. (https://nepalchurch.wordpress.com/2016/07/27/history-of-christians-in-nepal/)

Rongong, R. K., Panlook, E. C., & Varghese, S. T. 2012. *Early Churches in Nepal: An Indigenous Movement, till 1990*, 1st ed. Kathmandu: Ekta Books Distributors.

Roy, S. C. 2009. "Embracing Social Justice: Reflections from the Storyline of Scripture." Trinity

Journal. 30(1): 3.

Scott, N., Foley, A., Brooks, A., & Batchelor, A. 2014. *An Evidence-based Study of the Impact of Church and Community Mobilisation in Tanzania*. London: Tearfund.

Sengupta, S. 2006. "Protests against Nepal's King Grow More Violent." Retrieved March 19, 2020. (https://www.nytimes.com/2006/04/09/world/asia/09cnd-nepal.html)

Sloane, A. 2011. "Justifying Advocacy: A Biblical and Theological Rationale for Speaking the Truth to Power on Behalf of the Vulnerable." Retrieved August 21, 2017. (http://www.ethos.org.au/online-resources/blog/justifying-advocacy---speaking-truth-to-power)

Stott, J. 2014. *Balanced Christianity*. Nottingham, England: InterVarsity Press.

Tearfund. 2017. "Explaining Development: Umoja." Retrieved November 9, 2017. (https://connected.tearfund.org/ambassadors/digging_deeper/explaining_development_umoja/)

Thapa, K. B. 2010. *Religion and Law in Nepal*. 2010 BYU L. Rev. 921. Retrieved March 19, 2020. (https://digitalcommons.law.byu.edu/lawreview/vol2010/iss3/12)

United Mission to Nepal Strategy 2015-2020. 2015. United Mission to Nepal.

Wright, C. J. H. 2004. *Old Testament Ethics for the People of God*. Downers Grove: InterVarsity Press.

Wright, C. J. H. 2006. *The Mission of God: Unlocking the Bible's Grand Narrative*. Nottingham, England: InterVarsity Press.

Holes in the Basket?

Arlene Ward

An examination of land and social security provisions for vulnerable women in Vanuatu, and the role of the church in ensuring justice is administered.

Introduction

Every morning Leimas[1] rises an hour before the sun. She lights a fire, kneads bread, boils rice and cleans the yard. She works—at the school, in her garden,[2] weaving mats—all in a bid to support her young boys. Leimas is a single mother of two and she is afraid. Afraid for her sons who have no land inheritance. Afraid that once her father dies the three of them will be ousted from the family home. Afraid that they will have nowhere to go and be left without land on which to grow food. She is so concerned for their future that she has considered giving up one of her children in the hope that he will gain a better future if adopted by another family.

Women of Vanuatu, a small Pacific nation, are hardworking, creative and resilient. But this creativity and resilience is often drastically constrained by the extensive patriarchal structures and processes of

---

1   Not her real name.

2   Ni-Vanuatu Gardens are small subsistence farms, usually situated 0.5–1.5 hours walk away from the houses on fertile ground higher up in the hills.

inequality. Land for Ni-Vanuatu,[3] for example, is central to livelihoods and social security. Yet the commodification of land currently excludes women. As a result, women's access to land depends on their relationship to male relatives. This reliance on men has been often regarded as an expression of Vanuatu's wonderfully rich culture of informal care based on relationships, reciprocal giving and common *kastom*. Traditionally, *kastom* was exercised to ensure the social provisions of all members of society were looked after. However, the blending of *kastom*[4] with colonial and contemporary culture—such as urbanisation, commercialisation of land, and the advance of the cash economy—has only compounded issues of gender inequality. The small formal sector in Vanuatu combined with its largely patriarchal culture has created holes in this social security basket that has allowed vulnerable women to slip through into poverty.

For the church in Vanuatu, these holes present a challenge and an opportunity: to embrace our prophetic role, rallying for positive legal and social changes on the behalf of these vulnerable women.

SOCIAL SECURITY IN VANUATU, FORMAL AND INFORMAL

In Vanuatu, 70 percent of people exist in the informal economy, depending on subsistence farming and trading of *kastom* items[5] (ILO, 2013). The commodification of land and the spread of the cash economy, coupled with "the weakening of the traditional forms of social cohesion" present challenges for women, particularly in relation to social security (Government of Vanuatu, 2006:32). Female-headed households represent 13.3 percent of families in Port Vila and 12 percent nationally (VNSO, 2013:54). Many of these women who head such households have been abandoned, divorced or widowed, and are listed as one of the most vulnerable groups to poverty (ILO 2006:27). Women are also less likely than men to occupy jobs in the formal sector and therefore have less access to formal social

---

3   A Ni-Vanuatu is a native or inhabitant of Vanuatu.
4   *Kastom* is a pijin word used to refer to traditional culture including religion, arts, economics and magic. *Kastom* is passed down through oral storytelling and a practiced way of life.
5   *Kastom* items include woven mats and baskets, yams, chickens, and pigs.

security and cash. In some areas, engagement in formal economic activities even puts women at risk of tarnished social standing and increased violence from jealous spouses or other male family members (Jolly et al., 2015:37). With a lack of access to credit or business skills, many women are left with difficult circumstances under which to expand their formal social protection.

Formal Social Security

In Vanuatu, the combination of a small formal sector and the constraints of geography, and financial and human resources has shaped a culture that relies minimally on formal protection. The biggest provider of formal social protection in Vanuatu is the Vanuatu National Provident Fund (VNPF). This is a retirement fund, to which both the employee and employer each contribute 4 percent of the employee's wages (8% in total). Employees receive the funds when they retire at the age of 55. Women listed as beneficiaries of their spouse or relative may also benefit. The fund was established in 1987. However, a history of mismanagement and corruption has led to 4.4 billion vatu (approximately AUD $55 million) of contributors' funds disappearing and has resulted in some distrust toward the formal social security provider (Hill, 2001).

There are five other formal social security programmes in Vanuatu: family assistance and home island passage benefits for government servants; Ifira Trustees, which provides annual payments to Ifira clan members at the household level; the scholarship scheme for tertiary students; and the Decent Work Country Programme. The latter regulates and ensures benefits, such as maternity leave and breastfeeding allowances and provides the greatest social protection spread for women in the formal sector.

In 1995, Vanuatu ratified The Convention on the Elimination of All Forms of Discrimination Against Women (CEDAW). Since then, funding for gender policy has increased. The Ministry of Justice and Community services was created in 2006, which includes the Department of Women's Affairs (DWA), who chair CEDAW. This has helped to place emphasis on social policy change. This ministry, however, has the smallest budget and therefore little funds are available to implement policy and monitor its effect (Jolly et al., 2015:36). With limited scope and reach, the government depends on civil society organisations (CSOs) and traditional systems for implementation of social services. In a country where 82 percent of the population identify as Christian, churches play an essential role in ensuring that social security protections and provisions reach vulnerable women.

Informal: One Common Basket

While the formal social security sector remains small, the majority of Ni-vanuatu rely on the informal multifaceted relationship networks that bind people together under the *wantok* system. *Wantok* literally translates to "one talk", and denotes people from the same language group or clan. This system weaves people together through indigenous knowledge, socioeconomic exchange, ceremonies, land rights and cultural practice, which culminate in informal social security through traditional practices of "redistribution, care and community consolidation" (Ratuva, 2010:52). Based on collective responsibility, traditional practices include obligation by the community to look after the needs of all; a social security provision coined "one common basket".

Reciprocal giving or exchange plays a key role in this provision, both in bonding relationships and ensuring provision of needs when the going gets tough. Ideally this system ensures that no one goes without. As a result, maintaining relationships and ensuring a continual reciprocity of gifts and services remain an essential aspect of life. For women, their resilience to poverty, particularly in the face of shocks (price hikes, natural disasters, effects of climate change, death of a husband, etc.) depends heavily on these relationships. "Women risk exclusion from informal social protection measures if they do not fulfil social and community obligations, such as kinship ceremonies and church activities" (Jolly et al., 2015:37). Widowhood makes them especially vulnerable to this exclusion and can threaten significant social relations that have been "laboriously and continuously built up over many years" (Rubinstein, 1987:25).

Losing one's husband halves the effectiveness of maintaining relationships, yet they are still required to raise enough pigs and mats for ceremonies, funerals and weddings as well as for the bride price of any unmarried sons (Rubinstein, 1987:39). For older women and particularly widows, children form their primary support and care. Widows without children then are particularly disadvantaged (Rubinstein, 1987:33), as well as widows whose daughters have married away or sons remain unmarried. Women with no children may need to take on the work of a man, such as heavier gardening and tree climbing, which has the potential to damage their reputation as a "proper woman".

In this cultural context, land for Ni-vanuatu is a vital element to life and social security. It is the most important sociocultural asset on which to fall back on as a safety net. Access to land is essential for subsistence gardening and housing and provides important security when times get tough and everything else fails. Through land "a person derives not only sustenance but also social prestige and a measure of control, or power" (Bailey, 2008:69). Without it, one is completely at the mercy of the community.

Kastom land rights in Vanuatu run similar to those of ancient Israel, where land was divided between clan, tribe, family group, etc. In Israel, much of the land was inalienable and "intended for the survival and welfare of the families" (Wright, 2010:295). The same is traditionally true for Vanuatu. *Kastom* land rights are rarely for the benefit of an individual, rather they are intended for the benefit of numerous members of a group who are joint custodians of the land. Under *kastom*, land is communally owned and "everyone within the kinship network has rights to use it" (Van Trease, 1987). Those that appear to own land are usually just representative of a larger family group. *Kastom* presumes that the actions of these individuals will be dictated by the best interest of the group.

Women, Land and Holes in the Social Security Basket

Women's access to land depends on their relation to men, usually gained through socially accepted gender roles as daughter, wife, sister or mother.

In other words, a woman's social security depends on her ability to maintain and nurture her relationships with the relevant men in her life. Hence, there are some women who are more vulnerable than others when it comes to accessing land. Abandoned wives, single mothers, divorced women, widows and spinsters all risk falling through the holes in the social security basket that land access provides (Jolly et al., 2015:38). Increasingly, urbanised women are joining them, particularly those who have lost connection with their homeland rights and may not have acquired rights on their partner's land due to the relationship not being recognised by *kastom* or law. Without access to land, these women may lack the resources to grow food "and may fall into a poverty trap in which they cannot provide for themselves nor can they rely on others or the state to provide for them" (Farren, 2005:139). One of my friends fits this latter category. Landless, estranged from her family and separated from the father of her child, she remains in a poverty trap in urban Port Vila. Rent and food costs are high while the minimum wage that she earns is low. Without land, she cannot grow her own food. In a bid to establish and maintain reciprocal gifting networks, much of what she does acquire is gifted to those that promise future assistance, leaving her dream of purchasing her own land at a seemingly unreachable distance.

Matrilineal societies are scattered throughout various islands in Vanuatu: Santo, The Shepherds, Efate and North Pentecost are among them. In these matrilineal systems land is inherited through the female and passed to the males (mostly sons). There are claims that such matrilineal practices lead to higher status for women, reduced gender violence and higher levels of political participation. However, evidence from within Vanuatu and Solomon Islands suggests that within these systems men retain control over land use and decision-making (Farren, 2005:135; McDonnell, 2016:218).

In many areas of Vanuatu, a woman is given gardening rights on her father's land until she is married. At which time, this land is often redistributed to her brothers and she is granted gardening rights on her husband's land. Upon the passing of her husband, a widow can claim access to her husband's land. However, this tends to be dependent on "whether the family members consider the widow behaved as a moral and proper woman such that her claim should be supported against other male relatives, or male children" (McDonnell, 2016:199). Being a proper woman includes attending the approved church, deferring to senior family men, following *kastom* practices, meeting relational obligations, caring for family members and preparing for events.

Rodman (1984:69) highlights the vulnerability of widows to the greed of the powerful: "men of knowledge who are skilled at talking strongly and persuasively can exploit those who are unwilling to defend their land claims or who are less capable of speaking in their own defence." Childless widows are particularly vulnerable in these situations, as are those with adult children who live far away and are not present to protect her rights. Some may be invited back to her father's village, but if she has not kept close contact or if there is pressure on the land, her return may be unwelcome (Farren, 2005:137).

A widow friend in Efate spoke at length of the threats her land and house have been under since her husband's death. Men in her husband's family are attempting to claim the house in which she lives, while neighbours fight with her about ownership of the small garden plot near her house. She says she is tired of the fighting but she continues for her sons, so they will have land. She is thankful that her husband prepared her to stand up for their land before he died, telling her never to step away from the land when people threaten her. She hopes to be able to defend her land until her sons are old enough to protect it for themselves. Traditionally in her village, the chief would pair up male and female widows for remarriage and to look after each other. But no one listens to the chief anymore, she says. Her husband's family have suggested she remarry. However, she is too tired to look after another man and his children. She also fears that remarrying would mean moving to another man's land, certain this would result in her husband's land being taken from her and leaving their sons landless. She prefers instead to work hard at her job teaching through her church. She says that she is fortunate to have many foreign friends who help her out with repairs to her house and with other essentials when she needs it.

Legislation and Land

There have been many positive changes to laws in Vanuatu to grant equality to land for women, but there remain flaws in their implementation. CEDAW has been adopted by Vanuatu. However, it continues to be in conflict with the Vanuatu Convention, which gives equal status to cultural norms that at times contradict the equal rights of women. While a woman may 'win' rights to disputed land if it can be granted to a woman's son or brother, the hesitation to grant land rights directly to a woman regardless of her male relatives further denies women's economic independence. Even though "[t]he right to own, manage, enjoy and dispose of property is central to a woman's right to enjoy financial independence", it is one that women in Vanuatu do not currently equally enjoy (Nagarajan and Parashar, 2012:91). In order for CEDAW to be more effective and women to be granted full equality under law, additional work needs to be done to close the loopholes and contradictions that continue to disadvantage women.

While there is progress in adapting laws and policies toward gender equality, the majority of women in Vanuatu live outside the reach of the law. In areas where disputes are settled by *kastom*, gender equality legislation like CEDAW is not enforced. Others may be aware of their rights under laws, while at the same time understanding that articulation of rights is quite different to actualisation of rights. That latter requires "the ongoing support of community and institutions, including the police and neighbouring chiefs" (Nagarajan and Parshar, 2012:100). Without the assistance of law enforcers or backing by the community, decisions made in court are useless.

CHANGING *KASTOM*

Vanuatu is seeing increasing urbanisation as people move to seek jobs, education or money. Urbanisation has increased the vulnerability of women due to diluted clan identities and customary links to land. In urban centres, "customary law which relies on shared understanding between people from the same custom group is difficult to apply"; *kastom* usage rights for women to use custom land or share in the produce are often lost (Nagarajan and Parshar, 2012:96, 102). Further to this, there are minimal formal employment prospects for women that can offer them access to formal social protection (Jolly et al., 2015:39).

Moreover, with this urban social distance increasing a household's reliance on the cash economy, families are under greater financial pressure. School fees, family health and finding food among the expanding urban population puts pressure on land both for usage and commodification, in urban or peri-urban areas. The weight of daily survival and the limited resources available in urban areas have contributed to people becoming more concerned with their immediate families, limiting the extent of their communal responsibility. In urban areas, *wantok* links are often "invoked when the need arises and ignored when they become a liability" (Ratuva, 2010:53). While traditionally the *wantok* system was designed to provide for all, increasingly holes are forming in this social security basket through which the vulnerable may fall.

The commercialisation of land sold or leased to foreigners is the greatest contributor to social disruption in Vanuatu (Ratuva, 2010:54). Sale of land to foreign developers has reduced the amount of available land for local use and has generated increasing amounts of land disputes. Indigenous practices that consider land as communal are being contested by powerful men and entrepreneurs. Management of land is being more centrally controlled than it used to be and "the role of women in decision-making about land, traditionally afforded by custom, is being manipulated and eroded" (Nagarajan and Parshar, 2012:90). Many women are also being restricted from access to land and cash benefits from property leases or sales (Jolly et al., 2015:46). Powerful men are not always acting in the collective interest, with some being "motivated by their financial self-interest" instead (Nagarajan and Parshar, 2012:90). Modern common law carries the colonial and capitalist concept that sees property as something that is individually owned, a commodity to be bought or sold. However, it is the nature of *kastom* that land is inalienable, to be retained for the benefit of the future generations and provision of all.

The uprising of the commodity community in Vanuatu has exacerbated the unequal burdens of social protection. While the responsibility for care of young, elderly and disabled are falling heavier on women, men are increasingly absent from home communities in pursuit of cash wages that are often spent on personal consumption rather than household care and sustenance (Jolly et al., 2015:46). Close to 5,000 workers, approximately 82 percent male, head to Australia and New Zealand for six to eight months each year to take part in the seasonal worker schemes. While this scheme offers positives in alleviating economic pressures of high rural unemployment and providing families with opportunity to raise capital from which to launch small businesses, the lengthy absences of key family members contributes to disintegration in marital and family relationships. The impact that the spreading cash economy is having on customary ties and reciprocal support systems also needs to be assessed.

Gender violence is part of a grotesque outplay of the patriarchal dominance so prevalent in Vanuatu. Vanuatu National Survey on Women's Lives and Family Relationships in 2011 reported high rates of gender-based violence against women with the prevalence of partner violence being among the highest in the world (VWC, 2011:55). Some Ni-Vanuatu males justify domestic violence due to the *bride price* they pay at time of marriage, believing that the payment renders the women property of their husbands. However, traditionally under *kastom*, this payment is not a *bride price that procures women as property of their husbands*. Rather it is *bride wealth*: a social transaction that solidifies family relationships (Tor and Teka, 2004:29). Culture and *kastom* change, but not always for the best.

Many women face the difficult decision of staying in an abusive relationship or leaving, risking poverty, landlessness and shame. Many choose to stay. For some like Alice Karis, who died after a brutal beating in 2017, this decision can prove fatal (Vanuatu Daily Post, 2017). Police and chiefs often see themselves as mediators between couples, convincing women to return to their abusers rather than prosecuting the perpetrator (Biersack, 2016:307). Women also fear embarrassment and further repercussions from vengeful kin upon leaving. Rarely are perpetrators of domestic violence pursued in court. Some are 'dealt' with by *kastom* court even though the Council of Chiefs have agreed that such issues sit outside of *kastom* jurisdiction and criminal activities need to be dealt with under criminal law. Public figures further compound the issue, regularly making comments that excuse gender violence and assert the right for male dominance (Biersack, 2016:308). "Safe refuge for victims of domestic violence is a particular social protection challenge in a cultural context where women's access to subsistence-based livelihoods is primarily controlled by men" (Jolly et al., 2015:40). The inequality between male and females will need to be targeted for systemic change at all levels in order to maximise the safety and social security of women.

Kastom is fluid and changing. While this can be to the detriment of women, this can also be viewed as an opportunity for positive change. It opens up space for bottom-up *kastom* reform, where those in rural areas who bemoan the negative changes of *kastom* can work together with metropolitan workers, NGOs and national elite towards a "culturally legitimate endpoint" (Biersack, 2016:15). This fluidity of *kastom* allows opportunity for re-aligning *kastom* with the values of provision for all, further shaping *kastom* to promote the biblical principles of justice and gender equality in a way that may not have been present in the past.

In recent years, there has been work on policy change and the promotion of traditional *kastom*. "From 2006 the Vanuatu Government adopted policy to revalue the *kastom ekonomi* in relation to the commodity economy" (Jolly et al., 2015:46). Under this policy change, school fees could be paid using traditional valuables such as pigs, pandanus mats and taro as opposed to cash. As women typically create these items through their daily work, this system has conferred them more autonomy. They no longer need to rely on cash income, which they have less control over. This initiative has increased the attendance of girls at school and reiterated the value of women's work and creativity. Unfortunately, another suggestion under the programme to ban *bride price* of cash and return to the *bride wealth* exchange of *kastom* valuables was rejected by the Council of Chiefs.

RESPONSE OF THE CHURCH

Churches play a central role in Vanuatu, a country where 82 percent of people self-identify as Christian (VNSO, 2009:34). In many instances the church has been one of the most effective players in administering social security provisions to those in need. The Vanuatu Council of Churches (VCC) played a vital role in mobilising fast and effective response following cyclone Pam in 2015. The extensive relational nature of churches coupled with the biblical call to help others contributes to effective implementation of social protection measures. There are, however, remaining gaps in the church's delivery that continue to perpetrate inequality, high rates of gender violence and increased vulnerability for women.

In order to reduce the gaps in the social security basket that leave many women vulnerable, the church, following the way of the Old Testament prophets and Jesus himself, should speak out against both the domination of men and powerful elite, as well as the injustice perpetuated by the wealthy through mass accumulation of land. Choosing to ignore these injustices hurts not only the character of the oppressed but also the character of the comfortable (Stassen, 2006:171). Doing nothing about gender inequality and the resulting vulnerability of women to social security will allow distorted perceptions and a continuation of unfaithful ways in the church. Let this not be the case.

Land, Law and Policy Reforms

There have been many positive changes to policies, law and land reform over the last decade. However, there is still much work required to close the loopholes and contradictions in the laws and policies that continue to allow injustice and inequality on the part of vulnerable women. The church has the potential to play a significant role in encouraging reforms in institutions and government.

Vanuatu has a land tenure system where land that is sold is usually done so on a 75-year lease. It remains to be seen how Vanuatu will manage the expiration of these lease tenures. The Bible, through the Jubilee concept, provides the church with a God-honouring and just interpretation of land tenures that protected the interests of the vulnerable. This radical biblical model could provide a powerful incentive for the church to embrace a prophetic responsibility—encouraging land reform that more closely aligns with the Jubilee principles and, particularly when the first leases start to expire, assisting rightful traditional landowners to obtain just and compassionate outcomes.

The year of Jubilee was a settlement standard for the Israelites in the promised land (Lev. 25). Every 49 or 50 years, land that was sold was to be returned to the original custodians of that land. This process served as a reminder that the earth was God's, provided for the whole of humanity—not just the rich (Ps. 24:1; Lev. 25:23). For Israel, fertile land was the major source of sustenance and income, and became the focus of exclusion and oppression, therefore the "restructuring of land ownership would be a major form of redress of injustice" (Wright, 2010:291). Returning land at the year of Jubilee ensured opportunity for the indebted and vulnerable to attain economic independence rather than cycling further into poverty. Ongoing debt breeds poverty and other social ills, such as violence and crime. The Jubilee ensured that the debt of one generation did not condemn all future generations to poverty, and thus restored dignity and economic viability. Economically the Jubilee prevented mass accumulation of land by the wealthy at the expense of the poor while at the same time protecting equitable and widespread distribution of land that ensured social security for all.

Vanuatu, like Israel, depends on fertile ground for income and sustenance, and like ancient Israel, land in Vanuatu has become the focus of abusive power and oppressive exclusion. The church can speak into this issue by promoting land leases that more closely mirror that of the Jubilee principle. Under the Jubilee provisions, sale of land only really equated to the sale of the use of the land (Wright, 2004:203). Consideration will need to be incorporated in lease agreements for damage or degradation for commercial development. Clearer outlines or restrictions in agreements may need to be made regarding drastic changes to the land, such as limestone extraction, chemical use, or mass development that drastically reduce the potential for subsistence farming of land in the future. Currently land tenures are required to pay a minimal annual land 'tax' to *kastom* owners. Embracing a more extensive rent type system, where a proportion of mortgage payments are made in yearly instalments, would assist in ensuring longevity of support for the original custodians. Access to long-term savings accounts and opportunities to turn cash payments into a viable source of livelihood are both limited, creating a high risk of large one-off payments 'disappearing overnight'. Larger rent-type payments would help prevent the powerful in the family or community from spending all of the money in one foul swoop, reducing the vulnerability of women and children to poverty.

Pango Point is a substantial peri-urban subdivision consisting of prime coastal land near our home in Vanuatu. According to neighbours who claim previous custodianship of the land, it was sold to a foreign developer by a man who did not have legitimate rights to the land. By the time our neighbours were able to dig up the legal land rights title won under Australian High Court in the early '70s (prior to national independence) and carry these papers to court to prove their rights, two-thirds of the payment for the land had been made and spent. The final instalment for the land was awarded to the rightful owners. I have been told this family, who never intended on selling the land, was not given the option of recovering their land and was never compensated for the first two payments made to the corrupt seller. Current law protects the rights of the purchaser over the seller. Amending this by breaking lease payments into yearly instalments would allow more time for cases of disputed sale to be resolved before all of the funds have been paid to and spent by a corrupt seller.[6]

---

6   Promoting land sale laws that protect the rights of the custom land owner over the buyer would also be worth more in depth consideration, though this too may present many potential risks, however more likely at the expense of the wealthy.

The church should mirror the action of the prophets and judges of old. They did not remain impartial or neutral to oppression, but instead actively worked to ensure that the law was used for good, and that narrow interpretations of the law were not used to deny the rights of the marginalised (Mott, 1982:72). The church in Vanuatu needs to embrace this judge-like role in ensuring the laws and policies protect the interest and equality of vulnerable women and their rights. This keeps the law enforcers and national elite accountable to ensuring the actualisation of these rights.

Systemic Change: Kastom and Patriarchy

In her article, "Land Rights and Gender Equality in the Pacific Region", Farren (2005:140) warns that radical change in law reform would be "socially destabilising". Due to the strong male opposition it could generate, these drastic changes could end up being counterproductive for gender equality and women's welfare. Others like Rubinstein (1987) note that prioritising equality to land is an essential step in decreasing the vulnerabilities of women, particularly those of widows. Mott (1982:67) writes that biblical justice is "dominated by the principle of redress", which assumes that inequalities in conditions are rectified to ensure approximate equality in standard of well-being. For biblical justice to ensue, and for land, law and policy reforms to be effective, they need to be coupled with advocacy work at the community and civil servant level. This will involve a long process of encouraging systemic change regarding the rights of women.

The church can play a central role in addressing issues of systemic patriarchy that have resulted in inequality of land rights, high rates of gender violence and increased vulnerability for women. Most churches remain dominated by men and a theology that promotes or permits such dominance. The church needs to challenge this type of theology and address the inequalities between men and women. Genesis 1:26–28 proclaims that both women and men, without distinction, are to be the image bearers of God and have authority over the earth. Male and female are equal in value and worth before God. The idea of female submission with universal scope and permanent duration, an idea that promotes ongoing exclusion of women from leadership, decision-making, governance, etc., is based solely on their femaleness, and runs contrary to the values of God (Groothuis, 2004:316, 305). The issue of patriarchal dominance needs to be addressed both inside and outside the formal church setting via a multilayered approach including biblical and easy to understand messaging and daily reaffirmation.

Addressing patriarchal dominance will cross over into addressing *kastom*, which is steeped in patriarchy. Deep and ongoing discussions will need to take place regarding *kastom* reform to match biblical understanding of gender equality and modern-day urban developments, recognising that many aspects of *kastom* have been reshaped and misused over time. The church can work with communities, law enforcers and other civil society organisations to support women toward the actualisation of their rights that are being articulated in law.

COLLABORATIONS AND COLLECTIVES

The church's active role in ensuring social security in Vanuatu should continue to focus on ensuring that the needs of the most vulnerable are met and that they have access to resources in which to generate income. Churches can partner with other civil society organisations (CSOs), such as the Vanuatu Women's Centre (VWC; which provides trauma counselling, safe houses and legal advice for women) and the Sanma Frangipani Association (which provides support and livelihood training for people with disabilities). These partnerships could offer support, collaboration, shared training and networks, while expanding the knowledge and reach of those involved. Vulnerable women within congregations should also be encouraged to utilise whatever means are available to protect their land, whether formal (registration) or *kastom* (including women in community councils), while keeping links with their home village (Farren, 2005:140).

Promoting the development and support for church-based women's groups is a powerful avenue for collective action by women. Such groups have previously proved effective in influencing legislation on gender violence and family protection (Jolly et al., 2015:48). These collectives also provide a great opening for microfinance and livelihood opportunities, which assist in enhancing the economic independence of the women involved. These collectives should be shaped and encouraged in such a way to engage women of all skill levels and ability, with additional support or provisions provided to ensure that women with disabilities are equally able to participate. Responsibilities and roles within these groups should be rotated to ensure that all the women are able to develop in different skill areas.

The story of Ruth in the Old Testament also offers worthy advice for how the church should support the widows in their community. Leviticus 19:9–10 outlines the provisions for the poor, ensuring that they too can gain from the harvest: vineyards were not to be stripped bare or wheat harvested to the edges of the field, ensuring that the poor and foreigner (those without land) could gain from the harvest and be fed. Ruth gleaned from the fields of Boaz, ensuring provision for her and her widowed mother-in-law. Ruth and Naomi were both widowed yet Boaz offered protection from harassment. The church can use this story to consider provisions and protection for widows. This may be in the form of male support in securing land rights, standing up to harassment, providing gardening rights to church land for women who have been denied access to family land, or providing work opportunities and access to formal protection schemes. Whatever form this may take, the Bible is clear in its provision for caring for the marginalised, the weak and the oppressed. Such a concern is an integral part of the church's mission and raison d'être.

CONCLUSION

Social security in Vanuatu balances precariously in the basket woven from traditional relational, reciprocal and *kastom* land rights, and interwoven with formal sector provisions. Left as such, vulnerable women, particularly urban female household heads, face the prospect of falling through the holes left by these two systems. The church therefore has an essential role to play in tightening the weave on these holes and ensuring that adequate support is provided to prevent these women from slipping through. Advocating for systemic change toward gender equality by addressing both *kastom* and patriarchy will ensure greater security for Ni-Vanuatu women for generations to come. Supporting and encouraging law and policy reforms to better protect vulnerable women and collaborating with other civil society organisations will contribute to a greater spread of biblical justice for the poor and vulnerable in Vanuatu. Supporting church-based women's collectives and support groups will ensure that women have a place to work together for positive change in their own lives and communities.

REFERENCES

Bailey, Kenneth E. 2008. *Jesus Through Middle Eastern Eyes: Cultural Studies in the Gospels.* Downers Grove, IL: InterVarsity Press.

Biersack, Aletta. 2016. "Human Rights Work in Fiji, PNG and Vanuatu." Pp. 271–339 in *Gender Violence and Human Rights: Seeking Justice in Fiji, Papua New Guinea and Vanuatu*, edited by A. Biersack, M. Jolly, and M. Macintyre. Acton: ANU Press.

Bjornum, Yasmine. 2017. "Raise Our Voices Not Our Fists." Retrieved November 7, 2017. (http://dailypost.vu/opinion/raise-our-voices-not-our-fists/article_191976ec-2039-5b45-8cfb-9589272cce0c.html)

Dwyer, Maire. 2013. "Social Protection in Vanuatu and the Solomon Islands." *Policy Quarterly: Special Issue, Child Poverty.* 9(2).

Farren, Sue. 2005. "Land Rights and Gender Equality in the Pacific Region." *Australian Property Law Journal.* 11: 131–140

Government of Vanuatu. 2006. *Priorities and Action Agenda 2006–2015.* Port Vila, Vanuatu.

Groothuis, R.M. 2004. "Equal in Being, Unequal in Role." In *Discovering Biblical Equality: Complementarity without Hierarchy*, edited by R. Pierce, G.D. Fee, and R.M Groothuis. Downers Grove, IL: InterVarsity Press.

Hill, Edward. 2001. "Public report on the Vanuatu National Provident Fund Housing Loan Scheme Dec 17 1997. UNDO Government and Accountability Project." Retrieved October 31, 2017. (https://www.usp.ac.fj/index.php?id=13970)

International Labour Organisation (ILO). 2006. *Social Security for All Men and Women: A Sourcebook for Extending Security Coverage in Vanuatu.* Suva: International Labour Organisation.

---. *The ILO in Vanuatu.* Suva, Fiji: ILO (http://www.ilo.org/wcmsp5/groups/public/---asia/---ro-bangkok/---ilo-suva/documents/publication/wcms_366547.pdf)

Jolly, Margaret, Helen Lee, Katherine Lepani, Anna Naupa and Michelle Rooney. 2015. *Falling through the Net? Gender and Social Protection in the Pacific.* UN Women. Discussion Paper 6.

McDonnell, Siobhan. 2016. *My Land My Life: Power, Property and Identity in Land. Transformations in Vanuatu.* Canberra: The Australian National University, PhD thesis.

Mott, Stephen Charles. 1982. *Biblical Ethics and Social Change.* New York, Oxford: OUP.

Nagarajan, V. and Parashar, A. 2013. "Space and Law, Gender and Land: Using CEDAW to regulate for Women's rights to Land in Vanuatu." *Law and Critique.* 24: 87–105.

Ratuva, Steven. 2010. "Back to Basics: Toward Integrated Social Protection for Vulnerable Groups in Vanuatu." *Pacific Economics Bulletin.* 25(3): 40–63.

Rodman, Margaret. 1984. "Masters of Tradition: Customary Land Tenure and New Forms of Social Inequity in a Vanuatu Peasantry." *American Ethnologist.* 11(1): 61–80. Retrieved October 3, 2017. (http://jstor.org/stable/644355)

Rubinstein, Robert L. 1987. "Women as Widows on Malo (Natamambo) Vanuatu (South Pacific)." Pp. 24–42 in *Widows: The Middle East, Asia, and the Pacific*, edited by H. Lopata. Durham: Duke University.

Stassen, G. H. 2006. "The Kind of Justice Jesus Cares About." Pp. 160–170 in *Transforming the Powers: Peace, Justice, and the Domination System*, edited by R. C. Gingerich and T. Grimsrud. Minneapolis, MN: Fortress Press.

Tor, R. and Teka, A. 2004. *Gender, Kastom & Domestic Violence: A Research on the Historical Trend, Extent and Impact of Domestic Violence in Vanuatu.* Port Vila: Department of Women's Affairs.

Toa, Evelyne. 2016. "VNPF: A Commission of Inquiry 'Unlike Others.'" Retrieved October 31, 2017. (https://vanuatuindependent.com/2016/08/20/vnpf-a-commission-of-inquiry-unlike-others/)

VWC. 2011. *Vanuatu National Survey on Women's Lives and Family Relationships.* Port Vila: VNSO.

Van Trease, Howard. 1987. *Politics of Land in Vanuatu.* Vanuatu: University of South Pacific.

VSO. 2013. "Vanuatu Hardship & Poverty Report: Analysis of the 2010 Household Income and Expenditure Survey. Vanuatu Statistics Office and UNDP Pacific Centre." Suva, Fiji. Retrieved November 13, 2017. (https://vnso.gov.vu/index.php/component/advlisting/?view=download&fileId=2171)

VNSO. 2009. "National Population and Housing Census: Basic Table Report Volume 1." Vanuatu National Statistics Office. Vanuatu. (https://vnso.gov.vu/index.php/component/advlisting/?view=download&fileId=1996)

Wright, C. 2010. *The Mission of God's People: A Biblical Theology of the Church's Mission.* Grand Rapids, MI: Zondervan.

Wright, C. J. H. 2004. *Old Testament Ethics for the People of God.* Leicester, England: InterVarsity Press.

RIGHTS TO THE CITY OF JABODETABEK

Manu Ward

What right do squatter communities have to resist eviction in modern Jabodetabek? An analysis of residential rights in the city with comparative reference to Old Testament property law and agreed international standards, and an assessment of perspectives from a non-legal settlement on the city's margins.

INTRODUCTION

Greater Jakarta is reportedly the second-largest urban mass in the world (after Tokyo). It is a continuous sprawling network of human endeavour that covers the cities of Jakarta, Bogor, Depok, Tanggerang and Bekasi (abbreviated to Jabodetabek), the home of some 30 million people ("Jakarta", 2017). Generating over a quarter of Indonesia's entire GDP (Rustiadi, Pribadi, Pravitasari, Indraprahasta, & Iman, 2015), it is an irresistible magnet for Indonesians seeking economic opportunity. Every year, about a million more people settle or are born in the area, mostly in the satellite cities (Firman, 2011).

This phenomenal growth has historically been accommodated in haphazard ways, as various interests vie for space to participate in the global urban economy. Official city planning has, in practice, been dictated by large-scale commercial projects of wealthy private developers, and reactive government projects to address the resulting problems in the overwhelmed infrastructure (Harjoko, 2004:16). A feature of this ad hoc development is regular forced evictions—in 2016, there were over 5,700 families forcibly evicted in 193 separate incidents in Jakarta (Charmila, 2017).

Forced evictions are often justified by the government in terms of "urban renewal" (Harjoko, 2004:18) or "public interest" (such as flood mitigation works or transport corridors), and are primarily at the expense of the city's poor who have occupied land that is idle, marginal or with unclear title. They have often settled there in full knowledge of the ambiguous status of the land. In such circumstances, do they have any defence against forced eviction? Or is it proper that they are removed from land that was never theirs, so that it can be converted to its "highest and best use" as determined by neoliberal ideals (Cuadra, 2015:8)?

This study examines such questions from three different angles. Firstly, land rights need to be understood in the context of the legal and political situation of Jakarta. Secondly, this is compared with international norms for human rights with regard to forced evictions. Thirdly, the Biblical narrative is examined for possible application of land-rights in lawless areas from a Christian perspective.

The second half of this study is an assessment of eviction experiences and expectations of squatters personally known to this author.

RESIDENTIAL RIGHTS IN JAKARTA

The situation of legal ownership and rights to land in Indonesia is far from clear, and generally the government cannot be sure who owns what land (Cuadra, 2015:9). Throughout Greater Jakarta, it is common to see land marked out with makeshift fencing and a notice posted to announce a particular claim to the plot, based on a document demonstrating some historic agreement or exchange (see photo on facing page). Land ownership is generally not based on a single central cadastral database, but on individual papers, agreements and contracts.

In the colonial era, both English and Dutch rulers established the principle of domain (or the Dutch *domein verklaring* provided in the *Agrarishe Wet* 1870—"agricultural law"), whereby all land belongs to the

Making a land claim—An otherwise unremarkable and seemingly arbitrary piece of road shoulder is cordoned off with a sign that reads "Announcement: this is the property of Mr ..., based on Sale and Purchase Certificate number: C##/###/#/#.# on 7 March 1983. Area 50 m². AWAITING LAND PAYMENT BY REPRESENTATIVES OF BECAKAYU TOLROAD TEAM" (photo by author, Bekasi: 21 Nov 2017).

state unless proven otherwise (Soemarwi & Januardy, 2016). Proving legal ownership was the responsibility of the inhabitants, not the state. The implication was that common people were effectively tenants of the state or aristocratic classes, and could be evicted wherever they were judged to be illegal occupants (Jimayahatta, 2006:17–18).

This principle was modified after independence to become the Basic Agrarian Law (BAL, Act 5/1960), whereby land rights by default are owned by the State. It is estimated that some 40 percent of existing houses of the poor in Indonesia are situated on state-owned land. In 1992, the Jakarta Legal Aid Institute (LBH, *Lembaga Bantuan Hukum Jakarta*) claimed that up to 70 percent of Jakarta's residents may be unable to prove official title to their home (Jimayahatta, 2006:18).

The task of national land administration falls to the National Land Agency (BPN, *Badan Pertanahan Nasional*). Under the *reformasi* government (the present era after the end of Suharto's regime in 1998), the BPN began the Land Administration Project to register certification and reform cadastral information. However, the adjudication of land disputes and multiple historic land titles is fraught with confusing bureaucracy and contradictory regulations and is vulnerable to corruption (Jimayahatta, 2006:19).

On the one hand, land that has successfully obtained a nationally registered title with BPN is considered "formal" land. On the other hand, land that might only be registered at local government level is also considered "legal". This second type of registration is preferred by many for its lower cost and ease of process, but records at this level are fragmented (Cuadra, 2015:9). Furthermore, there is a complex array of different types of documents and rights that exist: right of ownership, right of commercial exploitation, right of building, right of use, sharecropping rights, right to occupy, as well as a variety of tax-register documents and different types of ownership documents dating back to colonial times (Thorburn, 2004:34). In the case of land disputes, where developers appear with unexpected proof of ownership that may not agree with local records, the poor often do not have the means to access the required legal assistance to argue their claim. Even when they do, proper legal evaluation may proceed too slowly to prevent their business or home being destroyed anyway (Cuadra, 2015:11).

There have been periods in Indonesia's history when the political climate has been relatively benevolent with regard to the residency rights of the poor. Indonesia's constitution (1945) and human rights law (*UU tentang HAM*, 1999) both affirm that all have the right to "settle in a house with a good and healthy environment". The government has acknowledged that it cannot facilitate provision of sufficient housing stock, particularly in times of great need. After independence, Vice-President Hatta in 1950 encouraged Indonesians to create homes for themselves wherever and however they might, a policy that persisted into the early years of Suharto's presidency after 1965 (Cuadra, 2015:9, 14). Following the financial crisis of 1997–1998, the government asked poor residents to occupy land alongside train tracks or other idle land to join the fight to save the national economy and ensure continued supply of much-needed cheap labour close to Jakarta's centre (Cuadra, 2015:10). However, such a climate of benevolence is not permanent, and eventually residents that once responded to these official invitations became the political scapegoats for various problems—flooding, climate change, traffic, disease, unsightly settlements—and face potential eviction, holding no legal rights to the land they occupied (Cuadra, 2015:17). In actual fact, a recent study finds that major culprits for Jakarta's "chaos" are large-scale mall and apartment developments. In the period 1985–2005, an estimated 3,925 hectares of malls, supermarkets, upper-class residential areas and private education institutes were constructed on land officially designated for green space, water catchment areas, or protected forest areas (Rukmana, 2015:363). Unfortunately, if authorities strive to restore the requirement for urban areas to have at least 30 percent green open space (according to Spatial Planning Law 26:2007; Soemarwi & Januardy, 2016), the likely target for clearance are not these high-class developments, but the self-built settlements of the poor.

Evictions have accelerated in recent times alongside substantial investment in much-needed public infrastructure. This has been enabled in part by the recent Law 2:2012 that streamlines the process for "acquisition of land for development in the public interest", that came to full effect in 2015 (Cuadra, 2015:6). Advocacy organisations, such as the Legal Aid Institute and the Urban Poor Consortium, have campaigned for the rights of fair process and proper compensation outlined in the law to be upheld. For any project deemed to be in the public interest, compensation is stipulated for any party that can demonstrate existing land rights, responsibility for land management, land stewardship for religious or charitable purposes, ownership or authority based on traditional law or customary rights, control of public land entrusted in good faith, land tenure, or ownership of buildings, plants or any other objects related to the land. If documents cannot be produced (which, as already mentioned, is often the case), it should be enough to obtain the written statements of two trusted witnesses from the community. Compensation should be made for the land, including spaces both above and below ground, buildings, plants or any other object or other assessable losses. It can be granted in the form of money, replacement land, resettlement, shareholding or any other form agreed to by both parties (Urban Poor Consortium, 2015).

Like any law, it can sound reasonable enough on paper. But the details of implementation have significant implications, especially for the vulnerable and legally illiterate. It appears that where there is disagreement, there is opportunity (but not obligation) for the governor to rework the project, after which the only recourse for objection is legal proceeding through the courts, an action rarely taken, or trusted, by the poor (Urban Poor Consortium, 2015). There also remains an inconsistency in that the government does not carry any burden to provide proof of ownership, whereas those being evicted are requested to produce certificates and documentation (Michael & Aziz, 2016; Yi, 2016). Furthermore, compensation in the form of low-cost apartments many miles away is often a poor substitute for the lifestyle residents are accustomed to. They find themselves with fewer livelihood options, disconnected from family ties, their children without access to traditional play, and, eventually, their inability to meet the relentless electricity, water and rental bills leaves them vulnerable to eviction yet again with nowhere left to go (Michael & Aziz, 2016). There remain many cases where no compensation is received by the residents at all, with years or decades worth of investment cleared suddenly in a single morning with unclear or zero advanced notice (Sheppard, 2006:2; and personal conversation at the scene of eviction for Becakayu toll road, 2014).

In their efforts to beautify, modernise, and streamline the urban landscape, the city's elite often overlook the value and character of informal settlements (*kampung*). Architectural professor at the University of Indonesia, Triatno Yudo Harjoko, calls the *kampung* "life *par excellence*". They are "a receptacle for a rural migrants' transformation into urban [life], which no other place in the city could instead accommodate" and "a container of urbanisation in which it allows most traditions of different ethnic groups to survive and transform into urban life" (Harjoko, 2004:6). Due to their unique mix of cultures and classes closely interrelating in mutual transition, they become places of inspiration for arts, industry and trading. Demolishing such areas not only significantly reduces the city's stock of affordable housing and wipes away a considerable portion of the informal economy, but also represents an intangible loss to the city's vitality (Harjoko, 2004:21).

One alternative to eviction and demolition in Jakarta has been the "Kampung Improvement Programme" (KIP). It was successfully launched in 1969 to transform illegal settlements into formal parts of the urban fabric and bring real urban development where it was needed. In its first five years, the programme cost-effectively improved living standards for 1.2 million people, such that the World Bank then offered soft loans to accelerate the scheme until 1982, by which time it had improved conditions for 5 million urban poor (Juliman, 2006). Critics of the scheme point to the increased land speculation by private developers triggered by the benefits of improved infrastructure and facilities in the *kampung*, leading to gentrification or redevelopment that eventually pushes out the poor anyway (Jimayahatta, 2006:19; Taylor, 2016). However, the change is gentler, more organic, and perhaps 140 times more cost effective than the current administration's preferred approach of clearance and resettlement (Juliman, 2006:2). The government continues to implement various forms of this concept in selected communities ("Beresin kampung, membangun kota", 2014). Although there are calls to revive the programme as the primary policy regarding slum areas, public involvement in urban planning, and indeed what comprises "public interest", remains limited (Harjoko, 2004:18).[1]

This discussion thus far has focused on evictions carried out for government projects, rather than private developments. Ideally, this is also the model for private projects and associated land disputes. Indeed the

---

1   The Indonesian word, *umum*, that is normally translated as "public", carries connotations closer to "general" rather than the sense of being "democratic" which is commonly associated with the English word. Similarly, the word for "government", *pemerintah*, is still more closely linked with its root word "to command" rather than being accountable to the people at large (Harjoko, 2004:18).

government, particularly at local level, is involved in mediating private land conversions. However, the discussion of Jakarta's situation would not be complete without mention of the *preman* that have actual control over certain areas. Originating from "free man" (Oppenheimer, 2012), the word could be translated 'non-government guardian', 'leader of bad boys', or 'gangster' (depending on the translator's perspective). These characters have acquired unofficial power either through personal charisma, corrupt collusion with local government officials, or thuggery, and maintain patron-client relationships to collect levies from traders or squatters on public or unregistered space. The levies supposedly guarantee the security of the client's occupancy, but more often are a form of blackmail and intimidation, and the arrangement carries no substance in the face of clearances by higher government or more powerful private interests (Harjoko, 2004:6).

INTERNATIONAL NORMS FOR RESIDENTIAL RIGHTS

In 2006, Indonesia ratified two international treaties (30 years after they were established): the International Covenant of Economic, Social, and Cultural Rights (ICESCR); and the International Covenant on Civil and Political Rights (ICCPR), which prohibit governments from unlawful interference with people's homes and guarantee the right to adequate housing (Sheppard, 2006:31). These provide similar guarantees, in principle, to the Indonesian law. They oblige the state of Indonesia to refrain from forced evictions, and take all measures to prevent their occurrence. Forced evictions are regarded as a "gross violation of human rights" (OHCHR, 2014:1) that directly or indirectly violate "the full spectrum of civil, cultural, economic, political and social rights enshrined in instrumental instruments" (OHCHR, 2014:5), often exacerbating the poverty of those already vulnerable and resulting in severe trauma. A forced eviction, according to international standards, does not necessarily involve the use of physical force—even in cases where residents demolish their own homes, such as the case observed in East Jakarta by Human

Rights Watch, where residents hoped to preserve building materials in fear of imminent destruction (Sheppard, 2006:31). Lack of title or property rights is not justification for forced eviction, as respect for human rights is independent from a person's status, including ownership (OHCHR, 2014:9).

International standards require that governments ensure that all individuals have a right to "adequate compensation for any property, both personal and real" following "mutually satisfactory negotiations" (Sheppard, 2006:33). A forced eviction is not necessarily justified by an administrative decision that conforms with national legislation (OHCHR, 2014:5). Only under the most exceptional circumstances is eviction against the occupant's consent allowed, for example to displace people from hazard-prone land to protect lives (OHCHR, 2014:5). "Public interest" or "general welfare" is not a sufficient explanation, especially if there is no control over such a decision (OHCHR, 2014:26). Exceptional circumstances may include persistent non-payment of rent without reasonable cause, discriminatory attacks against a neighbour, persistent antisocial or criminal behaviour that threatens public health and safety, or the illegal occupation of already-inhabited land (Sheppard, 2006:34). Even when eviction is fully justified, it is regarded as an absolute last resort action after all feasible alternatives have been explored with the affected community, and after due process protections are afforded (OHCHR, 2014:27).

Several high-profile NGOs are advocating for the government to attain and enforce these standards to which it has committed itself, including the Urban Poor Consortium, Human Rights Watch, and the Jakarta Legal Aid Institute. The task is not small. The Legal Aid Institute found that as recently as 2015, the majority of evictions carried out by Jakarta's government violated Indonesian law and commitments to international norms. Eighty-four percent were carried out with insufficient deliberation, 57 percent illegally employed the use of the army, and 67 percent did not provide a solution to the affected residents. This places the administration of Jakarta far behind many other countries, including neighbouring ASEAN countries, with regard to collaborative governance and expectation of public participation of non-formal settlements (Aqsa & Purnama, 2016:i–ii).

On the bright side, the recent spate of evictions has generated a great deal of media attention and public debate on the issue. Although Jakarta is still dominated by the power of capital and discrimination against the poor, evictees have demonstrated the capacity to make their case heard and thereby alter the prevailing public narrative. Researcher Muhammad Ridha points to the struggle of (ultimately evicted) residents at Jembatan Besi in 2003 as one crucial catalyst in subsequent improvements in government approach to eviction, including increased consultation and at least nominal provision of compensatory social housing (Ridha, 2017). More recently residents have organised themselves to file high-profile legal challenges to government evictions (Yi, 2016), and their struggle made forced evictions a major issue in the recent elections for Jakarta's governor (Walden, 2017).

RESIDENTIAL RIGHTS IN THE BIBLICAL NARRATIVE

Besides an appeal to domestic and international legal frameworks, citizens facing eviction may look for a more fundamental or religious basis to substantiate their rights. In a postmodern and multicultural world, political theorists such as Michael Walzer suggest that public ethics of justice are better based on "thick" narratives of historically complex and particular traditions, rather than the "thin principles" of universalisability advocated by Enlightenment rationalism. Thick narratives are what move and shape societies. Thin propositions made in the name of universal agreement are often left with little substance, ignoring and even undercutting a people's own tradition (Stassen, 2006:171–172). Similarly, priest and ethicist, David Hollenbach, argues that "each faith community must find reasons to respect the rights of others within the distinctive structure of its own faith" (Hollenbach, 2011:101). This study draws from the Old Testament scriptures for themes of land rights from a Christian perspective. It may be fruitful to examine the traditions of other faith perspectives for similar themes, but that is beyond the scope of this paper.

The Old Testament hinges on the exodus of the Hebrews. The Ten Commandments, called by some "Israel's Bill of Rights" (Marshall, 2001:72), begin: "I am the LORD your God who brought you out of Egypt, out of the house of slavery" (Exod. 20:2). In Egypt, they essentially had no rights. Subjected to relentless labour, arbitrary murder and violence, they were aliens without a land of their own. They were dominated by the myths of the Egyptian empire, in which Pharaoh, son of the sun-god Ra, sat at the pinnacle of an oppressive hierarchy (Watts, 2002). But the collective memory of God's intervention that liberated them to their own land later became the touch-stone of their aspiration to an egalitarian ideal, whereby even slaves and foreigners possess the inherent dignity and responsibility as God's image-bearers in God's good creation (Marshall, 2001:77).

For the Hebrews, the land ultimately belongs to God (Ps. 24:1), but is entrusted to the administration of human beings as its tenants (Num. 25:23; Ps. 115:16). Before occupying Canaan, it was agreed that the land be apportioned to the families of Israel in roughly equal measure, as their "inheritance" (Num. 26:53; 33:54). This was to be held in perpetuity as their unsaleable means of production, with the result of an "egalitarian society of independent peasants" (Mott, 1982:66). Furthermore, laws were established to prevent gross inequalities and disproportionate accumulation of capital. The most remarkable is the Jubilee regulations, which stipulate that every 50 years the land is returned to the original families. The effect is that when land is "sold", it is not a permanent transaction, but only sold in terms of the number of crop years before the land is returned at the year of Jubilee (Lev. 25:15), ensuring that no family could be "permanently dispossessed of the land it had inherited equitably in the first place" (Marshall, 2001:83). An interesting exception was dwelling houses within walled cities, which could be permanently sold (Lev. 25:30). Presumably in the ancient agrarian context, city property did not represent a substantial means of production, but could offer permanent tenure for the owners.

Besides Jubilee, the Torah laid out provisions for the landless that did exist in the community—whether Levite, alien, orphans or widows—so that they too had rightful access to the produce of the land as food for themselves. These included periodic formal charitable distributions (Deut. 14:28–29) as well as radical access to vineyards, standing grain, harvest surplus, and fallow fields and orchards (Deut. 23:24–25; Lev. 19:9–10; Exod. 23:11). Unless this access was abused for personal commercial gain (as indicated by the stipulation against the use of containers or sickles) it was certainly not regarded as stealing or trespassing. Such regulations were important in recognising the need for political action to protect the rights of the most marginalised to social and economic participation, and counter the "inherent tendency of all economic systems to concentrate wealth and power among the few at the expense of the many" (Marshall, 2001:83).

It is unclear how completely these regulations were kept, especially given the practical difficulties of implementing Jubilee. By the time of the monarchy and prophets, Israel had become manifestly unequal. A new aristocracy had emerged as owners of large landed estates, the peasants having lost their "inheritance" and with it their economic and social position (Isa. 3:14–15; Mott, 1982:66). As early as the time of Job, corrupt land administration is noted as one way the "wicked" drive others into poverty (Job 24:2). King Ahab demonstrates the extent of corruption indulged by the elite to steal a neighbour's "ancestral inheritance" (1 Kings 21). The prophet Micah decried the injustice of the powerful, who "covet fields, and seize them; houses, and take them away; they oppress householder and house, people and their inheritance" (Mic. 2:2).

When the land was finally forcibly taken from its princes by the Babylonian and Assyrian Empires, it was interpreted as reimbursement for its overdue fallow years during which its produce should have been freely available to the poor and natural fauna (2 Chr. 36:21; Exod. 23:11). Isaiah then looked to a vision of restored land rights in the "new heavens and earth," where its residents "shall build houses and inhabit them" and "plant vineyards and eat their fruit" (Isa. 65:21; cf. Mic. 4:4; Zech. 3:10).

Likewise, Ezekiel envisaged a restored Israel in which the princes "shall no longer oppress my people," letting them "have the land according to their tribes" and ceasing all evictions (Ezek. 45:8–9).

Today's world is very different to the largely agrarian societies of the early Iron Age. Certainly, there was no entity comparable to a modern megacity like Jabodetabek. Even the pagan spectacles of Babylon and Nineveh would be mere suburbs in comparison (Jon. 4:11). Modern urban societies comprise dynamic networks of enterprise in a transient population, with little need for permanently allocated areas apportioned to fixed family groupings. But some principles remain relevant for the economic structuring of any society. The Old Testament principle of redress pre-empted the tendency for accumulation of capital in the hands of the few. This is in stark contrast with modern Indonesia in which the richest four men own as much as the country's poorest 100 million citizens (Neate, 2017). Similarly, land was never allowed to become a commodity for financial speculation by the wealthy. Jakarta experiences rampant land speculation, which forces up property prices and keeps vast areas idly collecting 'paper value', whilst excluding the poor from its actual productive use (Jimayahatta, 2006:19). The ethics of the Old Testament demand that political solutions be put in place to address these chronic injustices.

A resident of Jakarta facing forced eviction is advised by the Old Testament narrative that, independent of their property ownership or residential status, wider society has a responsibility to protect their right to life. This includes the means for life, and all that entails, including the rights to decent housing—with particular attention to the needs of the most vulnerable who are otherwise without normal social security and family supports. As an antidote for the oppressive regime of Egypt, a liberated society will make available its "idle" land, and even the margins of "non-idle" land, for the rightful access and temporary use of the poor and the stranger, with guaranteed protections from the abuses of forced eviction. According to the Old Testament, those facing eviction in Jakarta are morally entitled to make such claims, and need not regard their use of non-registered land as sinful transgression or thievery—even including the non-formal electricity and other infrastructure that services them. Indeed, a population shaped by this narrative will be marked by a spirit of sharing and humble gratitude for God's provision, where the benefits of production can be enjoyed by all within the general locale of the community, such that "there will...be no one in need among you" (Deut. 15:4).

PERSONAL PERSPECTIVES ON EVICTION

The intention of this study is to gather perspectives about eviction from residents squatting on unregistered land in eastern Jabodetabek. It is a 15-hectare block, occupied by perhaps 700 families. A housing development had previously been started on what had been rice *padi* fields, but abandoned after the financial crisis and fall of Suharto's government in 1998. It continues to have unclear ownership status, and the land is temporarily claimed, bought, sold, and rented by migrant residents, families that historically farmed the area, and agents claiming to represent powerful parties with alleged ownership rights.

Many of the residents have previously experienced eviction elsewhere. This study carried out simple interviews with five participants. A table showing the interviewees is appended. Ideally, a larger sample size would offer a better range of insights. However, the efforts of this author were ironically curtailed by his own encounter with immigration authorities unhappy with his residence, as a foreigner, on unregistered land, to the point of threatening legal action and leading to an earlier-than-planned departure.

The interviews were conducted and recorded in *Bahasa Indonesia* in the period 14 to 21 November 2017. The questions used are appended. The interview format led to three areas of conversation, being a recount of past experience of eviction, expectations for the future of their current residence, and ideas for best government response.

Past Experience of Eviction

Participants offered a range of eviction experiences, and shared them matter-of-factly with little visible sign of trauma or regret. *Pak* Somad[2] and

---

2   Names have been changed to protect identities.

his new wife were evicted in 2004 along with perhaps 1,500 other families from what he called "government land" to be used for housing for the wealthy. He remembered being given one week's notice of the eviction, in the form of letters and posters placed in the neighbourhood. All residents were required to register their identity details to be given 500 thousand Rupiah per family.

They were given relief (*keringanan*), not compensation, but relief, to move

> from there and search for a more comfortable place, respectively, that won't be evicted again. It was up to them [to find such a place] ... 500 thousand was not enough, it was still a very big loss. But what can you do? Call it a loss and carry on. If you've lost out in the city, with no gain, you can't go back to the village. So we just live in the city and persevere until now.

He reflected that it might have been better for those with identities registered in the Jakarta city, as opposed to village migrants.

> For citizens of Jakarta (*warga DKI*) maybe the government might have tolerance, but everyone there were immigrants (*warga pendatang*).

Mama Nisa, who experienced eviction in 2006, never received any payment, but thought the "boss" of the rubbish-picking collective did receive payment according to the number of rooms he sublet out. She and her husband were given one month's notice to move, which she thought was probably reasonable enough time to find new living arrangements.

Pak Yusuf was given two weeks' notice. But the circumstances of his eviction in 2012 seemed to have been more formalised than the above. He had lived in that location for five years under the clear understanding that it was to be someday repossessed for the construction of apartments. He received a substantial payout of 15 million Rupiah to compensate for the cost of moving and resettlement elsewhere, although this still falls short of the real cost of the move, especially when considering the factors of a less central location for schooling and employment. Payment was apparently in accordance to the size and quality of the dwelling to be demolished, with some residents apparently receiving as much as 100 million Rupiah. He was, however, a registered citizen of Jakarta, and believes those with identity cards from other provinces were treated differently.

> They were regarded as different, because they came in from the village, without registered residency for Jakarta. Those with Jakarta residency [as indicated by their identity card] had to be prioritised. Those who didn't were only given around 5 million Rupiah.

Most of the participants suggested that those repossessing the land were acting within their rights. However, *Ibu* Risma said it could never be clear who the rightful owners of their land were. Some residents in her neighbourhood believed that they were in fact rightful owners, and after resisting eviction longer than anybody else, they received much higher payouts. She knew of a prominent community member who claimed his great grandfather had gained legitimate ownership rights, but without any written evidence, this claim proved ineffectual against unknown agreements between other mysterious and powerful parties.

> The new owners know more than us. What use is it to probe?
> All we can do is look on, saying, 'alas, once I lived there'.

She and her family experienced the same eviction as *Pak* Yusuf above. After eleven years living at that location, she received 7 million Rupiah compensation. Her story differs from *Pak* Yusuf's in that she remembers being warned four months before final eviction, during which time a large (suspicious) neighbourhood fire destroyed many homes and quickened the clearing process.

Future Expectation for Current Residence

All participants expected they would one day be evicted, and rightfully, from their current home. *Mama* Nisa expressed the common sentiment in the neighbourhood.

> We hope that this place isn't evicted, and that we can stay for a long time ... but that's not possible—one day it definitely will be evicted ... we just hope for enough time and compensation.

Several participants suggested that they would in such an event give thanks for the time they have already been graciously given, whether by God or by the eventual owner, to reside at that location. Though resigned to the fact, it was also acknowledged as difficult. *Pak* Alif said,

> We little people here, we hope ... the land is just left to be, for people like me. If we're evicted where should we go? We're tired of moving. Constant eviction is tiring.

Pak Somad optimistically pondered an alternative hope, that

> it would be better not to evict, but that this becomes our personal land with official title, even if just one house, distributed to those who don't have a residence, and that they are allowed to have an identity here. Then this place can be improved, with streets, drainage, approved rubbish dumping, good access for transporting kids to school.

Such possibilities are unrealistic, according to *Pak* Yusuf, given the increasing value of the land, especially given the recent opening of a new toll road nearby. Participants suggested that the place would most likely be used for housing complexes, or perhaps continue to comprise some green space, "lungs of the city". *Pak* Dani said they have no business in making such decisions as it is not their land.

Ideas for Government Response

When asked how they think the government should address squatting communities, it appeared that those with less education and currently working as rubbish pickers had fewer expectations that the government would or could offer any relevant positive intervention. This remains an untested hypothesis given the very small sample size, but seems plausible given how little government services feature in their daily life generally.

The three more educated participants, some of whom had more experience of the city centre, offered opinions in two distinct themes: better documentation, and therefore recognition, of squatters; and providing decent alternatives for secure residency. *Pak* Dani was most articulate,

> If the government wants to help the community here, and people like us, then record our data. [For example], how many houses? ... We just want to be acknowledged, that here there are humans. But our desire is excessive. We want to be formed into an *RT* [approved resident association], but that can't happen because the land is unclear... [In our previous neighbourhood there was no *RT*] but the *RW* [community ward] embraced us, oversaw us... If the government wants to look at us down here, don't use binoculars. Come down. There are lots of people. Don't stereotype us. We do have feelings. Clarify what work we do, and the level of our daily income.

As well as affording squatters many of the rights to government services (such as health and education) that they are often denied, strengthening the civic structure of the squatter community could offer valuable insights and innovations in finding more permanent solutions. Certainly, it would not take long to discover the strength of opinion against social housing apartments (*rumah susun*). *Pak* Dani calculates that the cost of setting up a new shack on non-formal land is about the same as only two years (subsidised) rent in a social housing unit. The former offers better access to community participation and the likelihood of much longer than two years' tenure. "Do they think we're stupid?" he asked, rhetorically.

However, they would appreciate help in being relocated to permanent alternatives. *Pak* Yusuf was sympathetic to the idea of BTN (*Bank*

Tabungan Negara—State Savings Bank) housing developments, which can be paid off at subsidised rates over about 15 years. He thought that these are generally more similar to the traditional low-rise *kampung*, rather than high-rise apartments. However, he suggested that, even if he received sufficient compensation payout, the bureaucratic requirements for accessing such a place would be prohibitive.

CONCLUSION

Jabodetabek is a modern spectacle of human endeavour, attracting hundreds of thousands of new migrants every year. They bring with them aspirations to participate in the global urban economy—if not for themselves, then for their children. Many of them have settled in the margins of public or idle land, forming the historic basis for the *kampung* within the city limits: unplanned settlements of self-constructed housing, giving Jakarta much of its vital character and earning it the nickname, *Perkampungan Besar*—Big Village (Harjoko, 2004:20).

And why shouldn't they? Even the government has pointed out, on occasion, that a centrally located supply of cheap labour is essential to the city's economy, and has in the past gone as far as to invite them to set themselves up wherever they can. Such an attitude, we have seen, can find parallels in the Old Testament laws with regard to welcoming landless strangers to enjoy the benefits at the margins of the community's production.

Unfortunately, legal ownership of large portions of the city (and Indonesia) is far from clear, fraught with multiple historic land titles, confusing bureaucracy and contradictory regulations. This leaves the poor vulnerable to the powerful interests of mall and apartment developers, or government projects of "public welfare", leading to the forced eviction of thousands every year. The great majority of these evictions should be classed as gross violations of human rights, according to the international treaties Indonesia ratified a little over a decade ago.

However, progress is being made, and the issue of forced eviction has been one of much public debate in recent years, particularly in the run-up to the March 2017 elections for Jakarta's governor. Several high-profile NGOs are advocating for the rights of squatters facing eviction, holding the government accountable to the aspirations of its own domestic constitution and laws, as well as international commitments.

The fact is that squatters *do* have the right to resist forced eviction. They have the right to full participation in decisions about the use of the land they currently occupy. They have the right to legal adjudication of all ownership claims. They have the right to full compensation for all losses incurred by demolition of their property—even if it is just a collection of plywood and old bamboo—and fair resettlement. In the spirit of the Old Testament vision of a liberated social order, society has the responsibility to protect the vulnerable and their right to life, and their means to life.

When the *kampung* are ripped out and replaced by soul-destroying apartment units or glittering temples of corporate consumerism, it is not just the poor that lose. The *kampung* nurture the organic soil of urban transformation and cross-ethnic interaction, and, as studies have shown, certainly should not bear the sole blame for flooding, rubbish, traffic, or hygiene. When the poor are included in the conversation, we may find that the "highest and best use" of the land does not necessarily look like the bland proposals of the elite, and in the process, discover more human innovations to the city's development.

REFERENCES

Aqsa, A., & Purnama, Y. 2016. *Atas nama pembangunan: laporan penggusuran paksa di wilaya DKI Jakarta tahun 2015.* Jakarta: Lembaga Bantuan Hukum Jakarta.

Beresin Kampung, Membangun Kota. 2014. Retrieved November 14, 2017 (http://mpi-update.com/beresin-kampung-membangun-kota/)

Charmila, W. A. 2017. "Forced Evictions Remain Rampant in Jakarta: LBH Jakarta." Retrieved March 26, 2020. (http://www.thejakartapost.com/news/2017/04/13/forced-evictions-remain-rampant-in-jakarta-lbh-jakarta.html)

Cuadra, L. K. 2015. *This Grievable Life: Precarity, Land Tenancy, and Flooding in the Kampung of Jakarta.* Master of Arts in International Studies: Southeast Asia, University of Washington.

Firman, T. 2011. "Population Growth of Greater Jakarta and its Impact." Retrieved March 26, 2020. (http://www.thejakartapost.com/news/2011/03/26/population-growth-greater-jakarta-and-its-impact.html)

Harjoko, T. Y. 2004. "Penggusuran or Eviction in Jakarta: Solution Lacking Resolution for Urban Kampung." In *Asia Examined: Proceedings of the 15th Biennial Conference of the ASAA*, 2004, Canberra, Australia, edited by R. Cribb. Canberra: Asian Studies Association of Australia (ASAA) & Research School of Pacific and Asian Studies (RSPAS), The Australian National University.

Hollenbach, D. 2011. "Human rights and Interreligious Dialogue: the Challenge to Mission in a Pluralistic World." *International Bulletin of Missionary Research.* 35(4): 98–101.

"Jakarta." 2017. Retrieved March 26, 2020. (https://en.wikipedia.org/w/index.php?title=Jakarta&oldid=809495960)

Jimayahatta, J. 2006. "Jakarta's Resistance against Forced Eviction." Retrieved March 26, 2020. (https://www.academia.edu/10999813/Jakartas_Resistance_Against_Forced_Eviction)

Juliman, D. 2006. "The World's First Slum Upgrading Programme." Presented at the World Urban Forum III, Vancouver, Canada: UN-Habitat.

Marshall, C. D. 2001. *Crowned with Glory and Honor: Human Rights in the Biblical Tradition.* Auckland, New Zealand: Pandora Press U.S.

Michael, C., & Aziz, M. Y. 2016. "'My House was Turned to Debris': Jakarta's Evicted Write Their Story." Retrieved March 26, 2020. (http://www.theguardian.com/cities/2016/nov/23/house-turned-debris-voices-evicted-kampung-pulo-jakarta)

Mott, S. C. 1982. *Biblical Ethics and Social Change.* New York, NY: Oxford University Press.

Neate, R. 2017. "Indonesia's Four Richest Men Worth as Much as Poorest 100 million." Retrieved March 26, 2020. (http://www.theguardian.com/world/2017/feb/23/indonesias-four-richest-men-own-same-as-countrys-poorest-100-million)

OHCHR. 2014. *Forced Evictions: Human Rights Fact Sheet No. 25.* Geneva: Office of the United Nations High Commissioner for Human Rights.

Oppenheimer, J. 2012. *The Act of Killing.* Dogwoof Pictures.

Ridha, M. 2017. "The Struggle of the Urban Poor Against Forced Eviction in Jakarta." In *Urban Revolt State Power and the Rise of People's Movements in the Global South*, edited by T. Ngwane, L. Sinwell, & I. Ness. Chicago, IL: Haymarket Books. (http://rbdigital.oneclickdigital.com)

Rukmana, D. 2015. "The Change and Transformation of Indonesian Spatial Planning after Suharto's New Order Regime: The Case of the Jakarta Metropolitan Area." *International Planning Studies.*

20(4): 350–370. (https://doi.org/10.1080/13563475.2015.1008723)

Rustiadi, E., Pribadi, D. O., Pravitasari, A. E., Indraprahasta, G. S., & Iman, L. S. 2015. "Jabodetabek Megacity: From City Development Toward Urban Complex Management System." Pp. 421–445 in *Urban Development Challenges, Risks and Resilience in Asian Mega Cities*, edited by R. B. Singh. Tokyo: Springer Japan. (https://doi.org/10.1007/978-4-431-55043-3_22)

Sheppard, B. 2006. "Condemned Communities: Forced Evictions in Jakarta." Retrieved March 26, 2020. (https://www.hrw.org/report/2006/09/05/condemned-communities/forced-evictions-jakarta)

Soemarwi, V., & Januardy, A. F. 2016. "FAQ Masalah Hukum Penggusuran." Retrieved November 14, 2017.(https://medium.com/forumkampungkota/faq-masalah-hukum-penggusuran-dda 003d430ea)

Stassen, G. 2006. "The Kind of Justice Jesus Cares About." Pp. 157–175 in *Transforming the Powers: Peace, Justice, and the Domination System*, edited by R. C. Gingerich and T. Grimsrud. Minneapolis, MN: Fortress Press.

Taylor, J. L. 2016. "Modern Jakarta Needs its Kampungs." Retrieved March 26, 2020. (http://www.thejakartapost.com/news/2016/01/16/modern-jakarta-needs-its-kampungs.html)

Thorburn, C. C. 2004. "The Plot Thickens: Land Administration and Policy in post-New Order Indonesia." *Asia Pacific Viewpoint*. 45(1): 33–49. (https://doi.org/10.1111/j.1467-8376.2004.00226.x)

Urban Poor Consortium. 2015. "Penggusuran Paksa." Retrieved March 26, 2020. (http://www.urbanpoor.or.id/pers-release/benarkah-warga-yang-tinggalmenguasai-tanah-negara-tidak-berhak-mendapat-ganti-rugi)

Walden, M. 2017. "Forced Evictions a Major Issue as Jakarta Goes to Run-off Retrieved March 26, 2020. (https://asiancorrespondent.com/2017/03/forced-evictions-major-issue-jakarta-goes-run-off-election/#FcXRphCTJj37BKom.97)

Watts, R. E. 2002. "On the Edge of the Millennium: Making Sense of Genesis 1." Pp. 129–151 in *Living in the LambLight: Christianity and Contemporary Challenges to the Gospel*, edited by Hans I. Boersma. Vancouver, BC: Regent College Publishing.

Yi, B. L. 2016. "Indonesian Slum Dwellers Challenge Eviction Law in Landmark Case." Retrieved March 26, 2020. (https://www.reuters.com/article/us-indonesia-landrights-slums/indonesian-slum-dwellers-challenge-eviction-law-in-landmark-case-idUSKCN1201QK)

Appendix A: Interview participants.

** The names of these residents have been changed to protect their identities.*

Name	Age	Home Village	Description
Pak Yusuf	40–50, male	Central Java	Security guard
Pak Alif	30–40, male	West Java	Rubbish picker
Mama Nisa	20–30, female	West Java	Rubbish picker, mother. With occasional input from husband, *Bapak* Nisa, rubbish picker.
Pak Somad	30–40, male	West Java	Labourer / Janitor
Ibu Risma	40–50, female	Central Java	Mother, maid. With occasional input from husband, *Pak* Dani, driver.

MASTER OF TRANSFORMATIONAL DEVELOPMENT (MTD)

Serving the marginalised in contexts of poverty and injustice is incredibly challenging work. Resources rarely—if ever—are sufficient for the needs that can be seen in the community, and the tension between what should be and what is can be paralysing. There are few easy answers, and many difficult questions. Yet there is a rightness—a calling perhaps—that can't be ignored, and which sees Christians serve the vulnerable in complex and difficult places around the world.

The MTD was developed with a keen awareness of the complexities of addressing issues of poverty and injustice, while also recognising that somewhere in the dialogue between rigorous academia, theological reflection and the lived experiences of those serving the vulnerable lies the greatest possibility of people being equipped in a way that is appropriate, sustainable and a bold declaration of the Good News. The MTD creates a "safe space" for this three-fold interaction to take place, and students who successfully complete the course can expect to have:

- a well-developed understanding and theology of integral mission;
- a sound grasp of the complexities of pursuing an effective development program in the midst of challenging social, economic and political circumstances;
- a thorough understanding of the roles and strategies of NGOs and churches in responding to poverty and injustice;
- a network of peers with whom to share ideas and support for the long haul.

The Master of Transformational Development is designed to facilitate and encourage effective contextual learning, carefully creating the space to wrestle with student-identified vocational issues and questions. The utilisation of web-based delivery together with 5-day face-to-face intensives in Melbourne, Kuala Lumpur, Cairo and Kampala enables students to study while remaining in their vocational contexts.

Their placement in small groups of 3-5 fellow students each semester, using internet-based communication, further enhances the opportunity for contextual learning.

In addition a wide range of "reflective practitioners" are employed to engage with students during the intensives as together they seek to address key vocational questions and issues identified by students during the 8-week reading phase that begins each unit.

Six units are offered on a 3-year cycle:

- Doing Theology in the Context of Poverty and Injustice;
- Economics, Development and Human Flourishing;
- Community Development;
- Biblical Justice, Human Rights and Advocacy;
- Climate Change, Justice and Sustainability;
- Leadership and Organisational Development.

Entry to the programme can be at any point in the cycle. A limited number of scholarships are available for nationals addressing poverty and injustice in Asia, Africa and the Middle East.

For further information visit:
https://www.eastern.edu.au/courses/master-transformational-development
or contact Steve Bradbury, Program Director:
sbradbury@eastern.edu.au

Eastern College Australia is a registered Higher Education Provider that provides teaching, training and research from a Christian worldview. It contributes to the Church and human flourishing through the lives of its graduates. Eastern is committed to providing high quality, government-accredited awards from Certificate to Masters, currently focusing on three major areas of study: Education, Theology, Arts & Social Sciences.

GRACEWORKS

Graceworks is a publishing and training consultancy based in Singapore, with a passion to promote spiritual friendship in church and society and see lives transformed through books that present truth for life.
You can find more of our books at our online store *www.graceworks.com.sg*.

www.ingramcontent.com/pod-product-compliance
Lightning Source LLC
Chambersburg PA
CBHW031457160726
47994CB00005B/2076